Nour Eldin Maglad

Population and Labor Issues in Sudan: Empirical Studies

AF141332

Nour Eldin Maglad

Population and Labor Issues in Sudan: Empirical Studies

Noor Publishing

Contents

Introduction

This book contains a number of research studies, some of which written while I was teaching at the Faculty of Economics and Rural Development, Gezira University- Sudan, and others as part of my post-doctoral research in population and labor issues at Yale University, and later as I pursued these research issues through further studies. Thus, chapter 1is published as a Discussion Paper in Yale Economic Growth Centre Discussion Papers Series. Chapter 2 is written through a research grant by Mamoun Beheiry Centre for Economic and Social Studies and Research in Africa-Khartoum, and chapter 3 appeared as Special Paper by the African Economic Research Consortium- Nairobi. The financial support made by these institutions is deeply appreciated.

Chapter 1is an attempt to quantify the various socio-economic factors that might be responsible for explaining variation in child birth and child mortality rates, and in particular, to ascertain the role played by parents' education in this respect, which from an economic perspective, could indicate the importance of the opportunity cost of parents' time spent in child care, especially that of mother's time. In addition, the analysis investigates the effect of household's per capita income on child birth and child mortality rates, and in the latter's functional form the effect of health services, provided by public hospitals and through some community health programs, is measured.

Chapter 2 analyzes the impact of factors in determination of wage changes, the emphasis being on the importance of human capital in wage variation. Hence, years of schooling and labor market experience are presumed to be important factors explaining the changes in wages. Thus, the proportional marginal change and growth in wages, or the rates of returns to schooling years and to different levels of education, were accordingly estimated.

Chapter 3focus is labor force participation of females and time allocation to market work. Participation and labor supply functions are used here to estimate the effect of prices and incomes on market participation decisions by women and to measure own and cross wage elasticities and income elasticities.

Chapters 4 and 5 are the result of research endeavors at the early years of teaching at Gezira University. They reflect a preoccupation at that time with questions of agricultural development and, in particular, with labor issues and economic efficiency of agricultural household labor. They address, respectively, efficiency of farming labor, and decisions of labor allocation by households in agriculture, through migration from rural to urban areas. Unlike the first three chapters, however, these two chapters are based on analysis of relatively small samples, a thing dictated by unavailability of data at the national level at that time, and the financial constraints that prohibited carrying out large scale surveys.

Chapter One

Fertility and Child Mortality

1.Introduction:

This chapter is devoted to an examination of the effect of parental education on fertility and child survival, and the interaction between child survival and fertility. Studies of other developing countries have found that education reduces fertility and increases child survival (Cochrane, 1979, 1982; Rosenzweig and Schultz, 1982). The relationship between child survival and fertility also plays a crucial role in the mechanism of the demographic transition from a high fertility regime to a lower one and has been investigated empirically for varied environments (Schultz,1981) but only for few African countries (Okojie,1991).

Sudan had a population of 20.6 million in 1983 and a rate of population growth of 2.7% per annum in the period 1955-83 (Population Census Office, 1990). Of this total 20.5% was urban, 68.5% rural and 11% nomadic. Completed fertility, measured by children ever born for women in the age group 45-49, increased from 4.8 in 1973 to 5.7 in 1983. However, the average fertility for younger women up to the age group 30-34 was lower in 1983 than in 1973. Child mortality, as in many other African countries, is high but has been declining over the past decades. The proportion of surviving children for women age group 45-49 increased from .73 in 1973 to .81 in 83 (Population Census Office,1990). Women education has been spreading but females' school enrollment still lags behind males' school enrollment. In 1985/86 primary enrollment ratio for males, age 7-12, was 58% while it was 41% for females (Educational Statistics Section, 1987). The aim of this chapter as set at the beginning is to explore how are these developments in the population demographics[1], of reduction in fertility and child mortality rates, been affected by improvement in education opportunities and particularly for women, as well as by other household socio-economic variables, such as income and health service availability.

The rest of this chapter proceeds as follows. In section 2 some theoretical background is offered and the empirical model is specified. In section 3 the data on which the analysis is based are discussed and in section 4 the empirical estimates are presented. A conclusion is given in section 5.

2. Theory and Empirical Specification:

The household economic model (Becker, 1965) has been used as a basis to study fertility behavior by a number of scholars (Becker (1973); Willis (1973); De Tray (1973); Schultz (1976a, 1981); Rozenweig and Evenson (1977)). In this approach, the household is assumed to maximize a utility function of consumption activities Z_i (i=1,....n), which are produced within the household using the resources (of time and market goods) and the technology at the household's disposal, subject to the constraints of full income and the time of its members. This optimizing framework implies that the demand for children is related to the predetermined exogenous variables which the household cannot vary: full income, value of time (given by market wage rate) and prices of market inputs used in production. Thus, if Z_c, Y, ω_f, ω_h, P_{xc} are respectively the number of children, full income, wife's wage rate, husband's wage rate and price of input x in child production, then

(1) $Z_c = f(Y, \omega_f, \omega_h, P_{xc})$

The partial derivatives of Z_c with respect to the argument can be signed under some given assumptions (Schultz, 1976a). Firstly, if it is assumed that the production of children is mother's time intensive, which seems a reasonable assumption, then

$$\delta Z_c/\delta \omega_f < 0 \quad \text{and} \quad \delta Z_c/\delta \omega_f < \delta Z_c/\delta \omega_h$$

That is, an increase in the value of wife's time would lead to a reduction in number of children conceived and it will do so to a greater extent than will an increase in the value of her husband's time. Secondly, the assumption of normality in consumption of children implies $\delta Z_c/\delta Y > 0$; that is an increase in income will lead to an increase in number of children. However, if child quality is recognized as an argument in the utility function, and it is assumed that the income elasticity of child quality is greater than that of number, then the observed relationship between number of children and income could be negative. Because the rich would tend to demand high quality children, this would raise child costs and therefore a negative relationship between income

4

and the number of children might be observed (Becker and Lewis, 1973).

In the following analysis fertility, defined by the number of children ever born, is hypothesized to be a function of prices, income and some socio-economic variables in the following way:

(2) $F = \beta_0 + \beta_1 E_w + \beta_2 E_h + \beta_3 Y + \beta_4 A_w + \beta_5 R + \beta_6 M + \mu$

Where E_W, Eh, Y, A_w, R and M are, respectively, the education level of wife, education level of husband, household's income per adult, wife's age, residence region dummy and child mortality rate. Education level is introduced to capture the effect of the value of time of the individual. Woman's age controls for the wife's biological supply. The income measure which is used in regression is permanent income as measured by annual consumption expenditure of food and non-food items (Deaton and Mauellbauer, 1980). One problem with this measure is its endogeneity. In the household, decisions regarding the woman's labor force participation in income-earning activities and number of children to bear are jointly determined. And since the woman's earning and consumption would be difficult to net out of the household, the income measure and the error term in the fertility equation will be correlated resulting in biased estimate of the income effect[2].

Child mortality is included among the explanatory variables since it has been hypothesized that fertility responds positively to child loss as well as the expectation of child loss (Ben-Porath, 1984; Schultz, 1969). It has been shown that, given an inelastic demand for survivors and unitary elasticity of expected cost per survivor with respect to probability of a child survival to maturity, demand for derived births will increase in response to a decrease in the probability of child survival[3] (Schultz,1976b). It has, also, been argued that child mortality is an endogenous variable and that the use of child mortality in the fertility equation would give rise to simultaneity problems because child mortality itself is hypothesized to depend on the number of births which a woman could bear over the life cycle i.e. a woman with a large number of children would suffer more child loss. Also, fertility and child mortality depend on many unobserved variables (Schultz, 1976a, 1976b). Olsen (1980) however, assumes that the cross sectional child mortality rate, the proportion of children dead to those born, is not correlated with the error term and can be used as an instrument to obtain consistent estimates. In this analysis child mortality, defined as death rate in age one to age five, is assumed to depend on the exogenous variables in (1) plus public program variables related to health and an error υ assumed to be normally distributed, which capture the impact of all other unmeasurable factors on child death

(3) $M = \delta_0 + \delta_1 E_w + \delta_2 E_h + \delta_3 Y + \delta_4 A_w + \delta_5 R + \delta_6 H + \upsilon$

Where H is a vector composed of health programs variables. The program variables which are used in the analysis are the availability of hospital beds per capita and services of the Blue Nile Health Project (B.N.H.P). The B.N.H.P. provides services in the areas of sanitation and combats water-borne diseases like malaria and schistosomiasis that are encouraged by irrigated agriculture[4]. The use of health programs in the mortality function only is justified because they are more directly and strongly related to combating and curing diseases than with birth control or the program of family planning services. Finally, the error term μ in the fertility function is taken to reflect the effect of tastes or biological heterogeneity on fertility and is assumed to be independently normally distributed but potentially correlated with M.

3.   Data:

This analysis of the determinants of fertility and child survival uses a sample of 2027 Sudanese households resident in rural areas of the Central state and one Western state (Kordofan), and four urban centers. The rural sample included thirty four villages located in four agricultural schemes that extend over most of the Central state and some part of the Eastern state. The households were selected by a multi-stage stratified random sampling where in each area villages are stratified according to the level of development, as indicated by the presence of services, with special emphasis on education, and a random village is chosen from each strata. In the second stage a random sample of households was chosen from the list of households in that village (see Appendix A for sample selection description). A total of 1400 units were selected in this way. In the urban areas stratification is based on geographical location according to the different income classes, using residential class as an indicator of the latter (see Appendix A). A total of 627 urban households were thus selected. For each household two questionnaires, one for the household and one or more for all married women in the household were completed. In addition, a community questionnaire registered the available health and education services, total population and number of households, transport facilities and disease problems in each of the sampled villages. For purpose of our analysis only households where both husband and wife are present are analyzed. This working sample includes 1807 households.

4. Empirical Results:

The estimation of fertility and child mortality is carried out for women with at least one birth. This restriction on the sample reduced the number of observation further to 1684 households. Table (1) defines each of the variables and Table (2) provides the sample statistics for the variables analyzed below. As Table (2) shows, the mean number of children ever born is 5.64 for all women, while the child mortality rate is 0.10. The number of births for rural and urban areas is 5.84 and 5.15 respectively. The corresponding figures for child morality are .11 and .07. Thus both fertility and child mortality are higher in rural than urban areas. The mean age of wife is 37.8 for all women. The illiteracy rate is higher among women than men, where 57% of all women in the sample are illiterate compared with 44% of the men. Older women are largely illiterate. For example 85%, 62%, 43% and 39% of the age cohorts 50+, 34-49, 25-34 and 15-24 are respectively illiterate.

Table (3) presents estimates of two specification of the fertility equation for all women and by region. In specification (1) the age of wife, the education variables, the logarithm of income per adult and child mortality are included (Appendix Table (B2) gives a specification where child mortality is excluded). Specification (2) adds regional dummies. Wife's age is introduced as a five years interval age dummy, with age cohort 15-19 as the reference category, in order to capture non-linearity in cumulative fertility . Fertility is significantly related to age of wife for the different age-cohorts as shown. An inverse relationship is reported between a woman's education level, husband's education and number of children born. But, it is the women's secondary and above levels of education which have a significant influence, with tertiary level of education having a still larger impact. Since women with these

7

education levels are more likely to be working or seek work opportunities for wages outside the home, the negative impact of education on fertility could be construed as reflecting the effect of the price of time for these women and consequently the cost of children on the number of children born. Moreover, consistent with the microeconomic model of demand for children, it is the wife's education which has the larger and most significant negative impact on depressing fertility compared with husband education's effect. The insignificant effect of primary level of education on children born is explicable in terms of the low value of mother's time as they face few job opportunities. The joint F-test indicates also that the wife's education and husband's education are statistically significant. On average a woman with a secondary level of education has 1.4 fewer children, whereas a woman with higher than secondary education has 1.7 fewer children.

Income is negatively related to fertility and has a statistically significant coefficient. This finding is contrary to the predictions of the simple microeconomic framework of fertility determination, where income increases the demand for children. The estimated income coefficient might not be measuring a pure income effect if there are regional or household differences in the prices of children which are correlated with measured income. The coefficient on income may thus be reflecting combinations of price and income effects. Since no account is taken of the opportunity cost of children or the opportunity cost of complements to children, a downward bias in the estimate of the impact of income is expected. It is also argued that the woman's decision to enter the labor market and fertility are determined jointly and since household income includes the wife's earnings and consumption the latter cannot be modelled as an exogenous variable. Fertility and income will be jointly determined and the error term and income will be correlated and hence the impact of income on fertility will be biased and inconsistent.

The Hausman test of exogeneity (Hausman, 1978) is applied to test the exogeneity of log expenditure per adult. Log expenditure per adult is explained by the husband's education, wife's education, husband's age, wife's age, the regional dummies and assets (see Appendix Table (B3). The variables measuring assets are categorical based on ownership and are found to be significantly correlated with income per adult and not correlated with fertility and child mortality[5]. Thus they are used as identifiers of the income function. The t value on the residuals from the predicted expenditure per adult is provided in the bottom of Table (3). The t-value in specification (1) indicates that the null hypothesis that income is exogenous is rejected at 5% significance level. In specification (2), which controls for regions, the exogeneity of log expenditure per adult cannot be rejected at 5% level of significance.

Child mortality is positively and significantly related to fertility in both specifications for all women in Table (3). The coefficient implies that demand for surviving children is inelastic assuming that the expected cost of surviving child is proportional to the probability of child survival. An average replacement coefficient of .20 is derived from the estimated coefficient of child mortality[6] (1.14/{1.14*0.10 + 5.64}). As argued earlier, if child mortality error is correlated with fertility error, then the response coefficient on child mortality may reflect in part the spurious relationship between observed child mortality and fertility. Thus the Hausman test for exogeneity is performed for child mortality where public health programs provide the needed identifying restriction. The t value on the residual child mortality in the bottom of Table (3) is -.97, in the preferred specification (2), implying that the hypothesis that child mortality rate is exogenous cannot be rejected at 5% significance level.

The effect of the regions in specification (2) shows large geographic differentials in fertility exists even after controlling for differences in household characteristics. Fertility is highest in the rural areas and within the rural areas the highest fertility is observed for the Gezira Extension (Managil) and Eastern Gezira (Rahad). Production in these two areas started lately compared to Gezira, and Rahad land in particular was developed and started production in the early 80's. Agricultural Productivity and income in these areas might thus be higher. The lowest fertility in the rural areas is in Blue Nile (Suki). This is an area which is characterized by the lowest mortality among the rural areas as will appear later (Table (4)). Urban areas do not favor a reduction in fertility. Outside Khartoum fertility is highest in Urban White Nile and lowest in Urban Gezira. Note that Urban White Nile fertility is not different from rural areas of high fertility. This area, as will be shown later (Table (4)), is also characterized by the lowest child mortality among the urban areas. The joint F-test indicates that these regional differences are

9

statistically significant at 5% significance level.

The fertility functions are estimated separately for rural and urban areas in Table (3) and are consistent with the previous findings for all women regarding the effect of the woman's education. However, in the urban areas, husband's education is significant for tertiary level of education while this level of education has no significant influence on fertility in the rural areas but includes only 5 percent of rural men. While secondary level of education of husband has a significant negative effect on number of children ever born in the rural areas, this is not evident in urban areas. However, husband's education is statistically significant in the urban areas when regions are not controlled, as revealed by the F-test. Once again Income has a negative and significant impact in urban areas and in rural areas in specification (2). Child mortality is positively related to fertility in rural and urban areas, but is only significant for the rural areas. The replacement response for rural areas as derived from the estimated coefficient of the child mortality rate and sample mean values is 0.23 (1.35/{1.35*.11 + 5.8.}). The Hausman test shows that in the rural areas the exogeneity of income per adult and child mortality in the preferred specification (2) cannot be rejected at 5% level of significance while in the urban areas the test for the exogeneity of child mortality is rejected.

The preferred specification (2) of the fertility function is estimated for different age cohorts and the results are presented in Appendix Table (B1). The negative effect of both wife's and husband's education and their relative impact on fertility is confirmed for various age cohorts. Primary education is again insignificant in affecting fertility. For the youngest age cohort, 15-24, only secondary education has a significant impact on reducing births. Few women, however, have completed any tertiary education and already had a birth in this age cohort, specifically 1.0 percent (Table (2)). Husband's education is significant only for the secondary level. For age cohort, 25-34, secondary education and tertiary education of wife are both significant in depressing fertility. Primary education and secondary education of the husband in this age group is significant in influencing fertility. For age cohort, 35-49, secondary education and tertiary education of the wife has a significantly negative effect on fertility. In this age cohort, husband's education has a significantly negative impact on number of births only for the 10 percent with tertiary level of education. For older women, 50+, completed fertility is negatively and significantly affected by secondary education level of the wife. Husband's education has no significant effect on fertility at all levels and education at primary and tertiary level is observed to have a positive effect on fertility. Note that the overall effect of wife's education is significant only for the age cohorts 25-34 and 35-49 while husband's education is insignificant in all age cohorts as indicated by the joint F-test.

A negative and significant influence of income is noted for the age cohorts 35-49 and 50+ while a positive effect is observed for the younger age groups 15-24 and 25-34 but significant only for the latter group. The positive income effect in the age cohorts 15-24 and 25-34 might suggest that women in these age cohorts are users of contraceptives, and by controlling for age the effect of children costs (in terms of contraceptives) is isolated from that of income.

Child mortality is positively and significantly related to fertility in young age cohorts 15-24 and 25-34. For the age cohort, 35-49, a positive but insignificant effect of mortality on fertility is observed. Thus the effect of mortality is positively significant in the youngest age cohorts where it is still possible to replace dead children.

Regarding the effect of residence one general pattern seems to emerge. In the oldest age cohort, 50+, fertility is higher in the urban areas than in the rural areas and the difference is statistically significant whereas in age cohort 35-49 the highest fertility is observed in the rural areas and the difference is statistically significant. The differential in fertility between women living in rural and urban areas diminishes as one move to age cohort 25-34 and for the youngest age cohort fertility is lowest in urban areas but the difference is not statistically significant. The high fertility in the oldest women in urban areas could be explained by the short durations or an abandonment of breast feeding and absence of other methods of birth control among this cohort (Caldwell, 1982). An alternative explanation is that these old women may have moved from rural areas to be with children. The observed low fertility in rural Kordofan might be explained by the continuous outmigration and the droughts in the last decade.

The OLS estimates for the reduced form equations of child mortality are presented in Table (4), for all women, and then for rural and urban women separately. Two specifications are presented: one without region controls and the other add regions of residence. First note that child mortality increases with the woman age linearly. An old woman is more likely to fall in the high-order birth group, where the risk of child mortality is high and hence to suffer more child loss. For all women, and by region, child mortality and parental education are negatively associated. The results for all women in specification (1) show that father's level of education had a larger and significant impact on child survival compared with mother's education at all levels when income is controlled. A primary level of maternal education reduces child death rate by two percent, which is not different from the effects of father's primary education. Secondary and tertiary education of the father produce a larger reduction in child mortality compared with the corresponding education level of the mother. Moreover, mother's education is not significantly different from zero as revealed by the joint F-test while father's education is statistically significant. This could be explained in terms of the differences in the educational levels between the sexes. There are more men with these educational levels compared with women in the sample. Part of the effect of mother's education might also be captured by income since the latter is correlated with mother's education. On the other hand the effect of mother's education may be underestimated if the program variables capture some of the variation in mother's education. Public program services of health and education in a country like Sudan tend to be made available together when they are provided.

A more restricted form of the mortality function is estimated where the program variables are excluded and the results are provided in Appendix Table (B2). In the restricted form estimates the negative effect of mother's education on mortality is more pronounced and is statistically significant.

The large magnitude and significance of the effect of father's education on child mortality may be over-estimated if education is correlated with some omitted variables that are themselves correlated negatively and significantly with mortality. If, for example the educated are located in areas where the mortality rate is low the estimated coefficients attached to husband's education will be biased upward. Farrah and Preston (1982) found that the regional differences in child mortality in Sudan are significant and persists even after controlling for socioeconomic variables. After controlling for regions of residence in specification (2), a reduction in the magnitude and significance of father's education is observed. Moreover, the geographical differences in child mortality are statistically significant and explain 3 percent of the variation in child mortality. In the urban areas mortality is lowest in Urban White Nile while the lowest mortality in rural areas occurs in Blue Nile. The highest mortality in rural areas is observed in rural Kordofan and Gezira Extension. These are areas of low provision in program services and rural Kordofan was subject to desertification and drought in the last decade.

The estimated coefficient on the logarithm of permanent income per adult indicates the favorable effect of a rise in income on child survival; presumably because it can purchase better food and health inputs that reduce mortality. In Sudan in the last decades, medical services have become increasingly purchased in the private market. The estimated coefficient of the effect of income, however, may be biased and inconsistent if income is measured with error or it is endogenous as we argued before. Based on the Hausman (1978) specification test, the t statistics on the residual from predicted household expenditure variable is 2.0 as shown in the bottom of Table (4). This is statistically significant at 5% level of significance. Household expenditure in the mortality equation therefore appears to be endogenous and other methods of estimation of income effects should be sought.

Public investment on health program, on the other hand, produces a significant effect reducing child mortality. The Blue Nile Health Project (B.N.H.P.) is associated with lower child death rates than the availability of hospital beds per capita. The favorable impact of the Blue Nile Project on child deaths could be explained by its involvement in establishing healthy and sanitary rural health conditions and combating endemic diseases, like malaria and diarrhea. One, however, needs to be cautious regarding the impact of B.N.H.P. shown by these estimates. If the services of the Project are located in particular areas on basis of better transport, the estimated coefficient may be overestimated as it would be capturing in part the favorable impact of these community variables on mortality. Health programs have a lesser significance than when estimates are obtained without regional controls.

The estimates of child mortality for the rural areas confirm the inverse relationship between parental education and child deaths which is revealed for all women. In Table (4), Mother's primary education is shown to produce 2 percent reduction in child death and is equivalent to a father's primary education. Both mother's and father's education are not statistically significant when regions are controlled. However, in the restricted form, when program variables are excluded (Appendix Table (B2)), parental education is statistically significant. Mother's primary education and father's primary education produce equal reductions in child deaths rate of 3 percent.

The estimates for the urban areas in Table (4) show that only the woman's age and husband's higher levels of education are statistically significant. Mortality is highest among the oldest women (10%). A negative but insignificant effect of income is observed. The income effect might be underestimated because of the inclusion of husband's education which is correlated with income. The inclusion of household expenditure could explain why wife's education is insignificant in affecting mortality reduction, since an educated woman in the urban area is more likely to be working and thus contributing to household expenditure. Secondly, in rural areas, mother's education has a larger and more significant impact at all levels compared with its effect in urban areas. A similar pattern exists for the effect of father's education in the rural areas for the primary and secondary level. The increased effectiveness of parental education in reducing child mortality in rural than in urban areas may be because education is more effective in circumstances where mortality rates are high and public health care substitutes are not as available.

The B.N.H.P. effect, when the child mortality is estimated separately for rural areas, though negative, is less significant than the hospital service variable. This could be due to the limited coverage of the Blue Nile scheme and to the differential impact which these services might have in the different socio-economic groups. Studies of child mortality have found that the benefits from public health-sanitation services depend on mother's education (Schultz, 1984; Rosenzweig and Schultz, 1982). If the uneducated women are disproportionately using the hospital services, and since these are the groups which suffer most from child death, the effect of hospital service would be expected to be larger and more significant on child death reduction compared to that of the Blue Nile Health Scheme. Uneducated women are more likely than educated women to use hospitals, which require waiting in long queues and travel time, because the opportunity value of their time is low compared to that of the educated. One test of the interaction between education and program service in rural areas shows that the uneducated benefit more from hospitals in terms of child death reduction compared with the educated (see Appendix Table(B4)). A negative sign on the interaction terms between mother's education and the Blue Nile Project indicates that the services of this program which are largely of sanitary and protective medicine are complementary to mother's education. Note that in the urban areas estimates of child mortality, in Table (4), hospital services are not statistically significant in influencing mortality, implying that there is no basis for identifying mortality in urban areas.

Hausman (1978) specification test indicated that in the fertility equation when regions are controlled, in Table (3) specification (2), the hypothesis of exogeneity of income is not rejected. The hypothesis of exogeneity of child mortality is also accepted for all and rural sample but not for the urban sample, in which mortality cannot be identified through the health programs as noted above. The specification test however does not support the hypothesis that income is exogenous in the mortality function for total sample and rural sample, Table (4). For this reason Two Stage Least Squares (TSLS) are sought, and the mortality function is estimated for all and rural sample, where income is instrumented on some of the productive assets of the household as shown in the Appendix Table (B3). TSLS are also used to estimate the fertility equation where child mortality is instrumented on the health program variables for all women and the sample of rural women. The results of estimation by TSLS are presented in Table (5).

The TSLS estimates for child mortality in Table (5) are consistent with those obtained previously as far as how parental education affects child survival. This time however, for all women, the effect of husband's primary education is only one fifth the effect of a primary maternal education. The magnitude and the significance of husband's education are reduced considerably in these estimates. Income now has a larger effect on child mortality and highly significant compared with OLS estimates. Note that while the health services have the expected effect on child survival, they are less significant. Husband's education is no longer significant as a determinant of reduction in child mortality. Since husband's education works through income the effect of father's education may be underestimated. The variables which exert a significant influence on child mortality are the woman's age, areas of residence, income and to some extent the hospital services. The TSLS estimates of fertility confirm the direction and the importance of the wife's education on fertility behavior. A higher estimate of the effect of mortality on fertility is observed this time though with a lower t-value. The effect of income is reduced and seems to work indirectly through its effect on child mortality. The estimates for all women show that although husband's education is negatively related to fertility it is not statistically significant as reported with OLS estimates. The variables which influence fertility significantly are the wife's age, wife's education, income and areas of residence.

5.   Summary:

This chapter examined the determinants of fertility in the context of the microeconomic model of household production. It also considered the factors affecting child mortality. The evidence indicates that wife's age and education, husband's education and household income are important factors in explaining family size and child mortality. These factors explain more than 40 percent of the total variation in fertility for all women and above 50 percent of urban fertility variation. Also, 8 percent to 10 percent of the variance in child mortality is explained by these factors.

Child mortality is found to be inversely associated with parental education. In regressions where only parental education and income are included, OLS estimates for all women indicate that maternal primary education brings a reduction of 3% in average child mortality. With an average child mortality rate of .10 this implies a reduction of 3 per 1000. A similar effect is observed for father's primary education. Though secondary education and tertiary education of parents also produces a reduction in child mortality it is the father's secondary education and tertiary education which has the large and significant effect.

In the rural areas it is the mother's education which is more important in influencing child mortality while in the urban areas the father's education is more important. Thus in the rural areas, a primary education level of the mother brings a reduction of almost 3% in average child mortality. In the urban areas, secondary education and tertiary education of the father brings a reduction in child mortality of 3% and 7% respectively but only tertiary education is highly significant. When program and regional controls are introduced the impact of parental education is reduced, and mother's education becomes statistically insignificant.

Government health services are indicated to improve the chances of child survival. Thus the sample average hospital beds per capita (curative medicine) is shown to be associated with a reduction of 4% in average child mortality, which is twice the effect of the provision of Blue Nile Health Project services (largely of preventive medicine). The services of the latter are largely confined to the rural areas and the estimates imply that they tend to benefit those with high income.

The computed average income elasticity of child death is - .1, indicating that doubling income from its sample mean would reduce child mortality by .01. Because of the endogeneity of income in the mortality function TSLS are sought to estimate the effect of income. TSLS overall estimates indicate that income produces a larger and more significant effect on child mortality. Based on TSLS estimates, an income elasticity of child death of - .5 and - .7 is estimated for all women and rural women, respectively. Thus a doubling of income would bring a reduction of .05 on average child mortality. Also, TSLS estimates of father education effect are statistically insignificant. The factors which significantly influence child mortality in TSLS regressions are wife's age, income, hospital services and areas of residence.

In the fertility function, parental education, which is taken as a proxy for the opportunity cost of time, is found to affect demand for children negatively and significantly. Mother's education at secondary and tertiary level is found to produce the largest and most significant reduction in fertility. A woman with secondary level of education would have 25% fewer births (1.4 fewer children) than the average (5.6 children) whereas a woman with tertiary education has 30% fewer children (1.7 children). Primary education of a mother is associated with a 4% reduction in average fertility, but is only weakly significant. Fertility differs significantly by area of residence, and after controlling for education urban residence does not seem to favor reductions in fertility.

The income elasticity of demand for children is -.03, implying that doubling the income from its sample mean would reduce fertility by 3%. The income elasticity in rural areas is equal to the overall average of -.03 whereas urban income elasticity is higher, -.04. The negative income effect on fertility may reflect the high cost of children as a consequence of parents' desire for high quality of children through investment in schooling. Over all women, using OLS estimates, the child replacement effect is .20 whereas in rural areas a child mortality replacement effect is .23. This implies that for rural areas, where child mortality is 11 percent, a reduction of fifty percent in child death would reduce average fertility from 5.84 to 5.77 children. That is for every 100 families 7 fewer children would be born.

Notes:

1. Some recent data on Sudan's population are available. The 2008 Population Census revealed that population of North Sudan amounted to over 30 million, and as of July 2014 it is estimated at 35.4; population growth rate has declined from 3.2 in 1990 to a current value of 2.4 or even lower rate of 1.83. Infant mortality rate is estimated at 91 in 1000 birth rate and declined to 64 per 1000 births in 2010 while total fertility rate continued to decline from 5.81 in 1990 to 4.6 in 2010 (the latter estimates includes Southern Sudan) (http//en.m. Wikipedia.org)

2. It was not possible to determine annual current income precisely. Although income from wages and salaries, income transfers and home production are observed, the value of services from durable goods and the imputed rent of an owner-occupant house could not be measured for all units. Imputed rent could be determined only for urban residents. Also for some households, where the head is retired or unemployed, none of the sources of current income are reported. The estimates of current income would probably suffer from sample selection bias (Heckman, 1979).

3 If B^d is the number of births parents want, then it can be expressed as

$$B^d = (1/p)^\gamma F^s(x,\mu)$$

where p is the expected child survival probability and $F^s(x,\mu)$ is the number of surviving children that parents desire, which depends on a set of socio-economic factors, x, which includes the cost of surviving child, c(p),and tastes distributed at random, μ. Assuming $\gamma = 1$, and differentiating with respect to p,

$$\delta B^d/\delta p = (1/p) (\delta F^s/\delta c)(\delta c/\delta p) - F^s/p^2$$

Thus

$$(\delta B^d/\delta p)(p/B^d) = [(\delta F^s/\delta c)(c/F^s)][(\delta c/\delta p)(p/c)] - 1$$

or $\eta_{bp} = \eta_{sc}\eta_{cp} - 1$. Both η_{sc} and η_{cp} are negative and if their product is less than unity, the elasticity of demand for births with respect to the probability of survival, η_{bp}, will be negative. If the elasticity of the expected cost per survival with respect to the probability of child survival to maturity, η_{cp}, is assumed to be unitary then $|\eta_{sc}| < 1$, that is, demand for surviving children is inelastic.

4. The Blue Nile Health Project (BNHP) is a joint venture between the Sudan Government and the World Health Organization (WHO). The program was launched in 1979 and began its operations in 1980. The B.N.H.P. has been successful in establishing improved sanitation and health education services. Safe water supplies, through the installation of deep bore wells, shallow wells with hand pumps, and construction of Horizontal Flow Roughening/Slow Sand Filters (HFR/SSF) with hand pumps, have been made available in all the villages covered by the project. In addition latrine slabs have been provided for all households in the covered areas (B.N.H.P., 1989). In fact when the source of water for the community in rural areas is statistically controlled, the presence of the Blue Nile scheme becomes insignificant as a determinant of child survival.

5. The assets which are distinguished as identifiers of income are ownership of vehicles used for commercial purposes like pick-up trucks and Lorries. Ownership of a shop or grocery and ownership of small scale productive enterprises like bakeries, oil mills or flour mills. The farm machineries are things like tractors and harvesters. All these categories are used for productive purposes and they do not distinguish the household as being engaged in any one particular occupation e.g. farm jobs or commercial and services occupation. More often income from the main occupation is supplemented by engagement in secondary jobs through these activities.

6. If the mortality rate $M = D/F$, defined as the number proportion of dead children, D, over those born, F, then replacement rate is obtained from an OLS as follows;

$$\delta F/\delta D = \beta_6 /[\ \beta_6 M + F\ ],$$

Where F and M are the average values for the sample.

REFERENCES

Becker, G.S. (1965), "A Theory of the Allocation of Time" Economic Journal, vol.
    75, pp. 493-517.

_____ And H.G.Lewis (1973), "On the Interaction between Quantity and Quality   of Children," Journal of Political Economy, vol.81, 11, Supplement,   March/April, pp. s279-288.

Ben-Porath, Y. (1980), "Child Mortality and Fertility: Issues in the Demographic   Transition of a Migrant Population," in R.A.Easterlin, Population and   Economic Change in Developing Countries, Chicago: University of Chicago   Press.

B. N. H. P. (1989), The Blue Nile Health Project Annual Report 1989, Ministry of   Health, The Republic of Sudan.

Caldwell, J. (1982), Theory of Fertility Decline, Academic Press.

Cochrane, S.H. (1979), "Fertility and Education: What do we Really Know?" World   Bank Staff Occasional Papers No. 26, Baltimore: John Hopkins University   Press.

Cochrane, S.H. et.al (1982), "Parental Education and Child Health: Intracountry Evidence," Health Policy and Education, vol. 2, pp. 213-249.

Detray, D.N. (1973), "Child Quality and the Demand for Children," Journal of
    Political Economy, vol. 81, Supplement, March/April, s70-95.

Deaton, A. and J.Muellbauer (1980), Economics and Consumer Behavior. New York: Cambridge University Press.

Educational Statistics Section (1987), Educational Statistics: Academic Year
    1985/86, Ministry of Education, the Republic of Sudan, Khartoum.

Farah, A.A. and S.H.Preston (1982), "Child Mortality Differentials in Sudan" Population and Development Review, vol. 8, No. 2, pp. 365-83.

Heckman, J. (1979), "Sample Selection as Specification Error," Econometrica, vol. 47, No. 1, pp. 153-161.

Hausman, J. (1978), "Specification Tests in Econometrics," Econometrica, vol. 47, No. 1, pp. 153-162.

Okojie, C.E.E. (1991), "Fertility Response to Child Survival in Nigeria: An Analysis of Micro data from Bendel State," in T.P.Schultz (ed.), Research in Population Economics, vol. 7, Greenwich, CT: JAI Press.

Olsen, R.J. (1980), "Estimating the Effect of Child Mortality on the Number of Births," Demography, vol. 17, No. 4, pp. 429-443.

Maglad, N.E., "Fertility in Rural Sudan: The Effect of Landholding and Child Mortality," forthcoming, Economic Development and Cultural Change.

Rosenzweig, M. and R.E.Evenson (1977), "Fertility, Schooling and Economic Contribution of Children in Rural India," Econometrica, vol. 45, No. 5, pp. 1065-79.

_____ And T.P.Schultz (1982), "Child Mortality and Fertility in Columbia: Individual and Community Effects," Health Policy and Education, vol. 2, pp. 305-48.

Population Census Office (1990), Population and Housing Census of the Sudan 1883, Ministry of Finance and Economic Planning, the Republic of Sudan, Khartoum.

Schultz, T.P. (1969), "An Economic Model of Family Planning and Fertility," Journal of Political Economy, vol.77, No. 2, pp. 153-80.

_____ (1976a), "Determinants of Fertility: A Micro-economic Model of Choice," in Ansely Coale (ed.), <u>Economic Factors in Population Growth</u>. New   York: Halstead Press, pp. 89-124.

_____ (1976b), "Interrelationship between Mortality and Fertility," in R.G. Ridker, <u>Population and Development</u>. Baltimore: The John Hopkins University   Press.

_____ (1981), <u>Economics of Population</u>, Addison-Wesley Publishing Co.

_____ (1984), "Studying the Impact of Household Economics and Community variables on Child Mortality," in W.H.Mosley and L.C. Chen (ed.), Child Survival, <u>Population and Development Review</u>, Supplement to vol. 10.

Table (1): Description of Variables

Variable	Definition
Endogenous Household	
Children Ever Born	Number of Live Birth
Child Mortality	Proportion of Live Birth Dead
Exogenous Household	
Woman's Age	Age of Wife's in Years
Wife's Education:	
Primary	Dummy = 1 if Wife has Primary Schooling
Secondary	Dummy = 1 if Wife has Secondary Schooling
Tertiary	Dummy = 1 if Wife has above Secondary Schooling
Husband's Education:	
Primary	Dummy = 1 if Husband has Primary Schooling
Secondary	Dummy = 1 if Husband has Secondary Schooling
Tertiary	Dummy = 1 if Husband has above Secondary Schooling
Log(Income/adult)	The value of annual consumption expenditure on food and nonfood items, including the value of goods used for consumption from own farm production, in thousand pounds, divided by adults, 15 years and over, in household and expressed in natural logarithm. The variable is potentially endogenous.

Exogenous Community

Programs:

Hospital Beds	Number of Hospital Beds per Ten Thousand in Area Council
Blue Nile Health Project(B.N.H.P)	Dummy = 1 if village is under Blue Nile Health Project

Regions:

Rural/Gezira Main	Dummy = 1 if residence is Main Gezira

Rural/Gezira Extension	Dummy = 1 if residence is Managil
Rural/Eastern Gezira	Dummy = 1 if residence is Rahad
Rural/Blue Nile	Dummy = 1 if residence is Elsuki
Rural/Kordofan	Dummy = 1 if residence is Kordofan
Urban/Gezira	Dummy = 1 if residence is Wadmedani
Urban/Blue Nile	Dummy = 1 if residence is Sennar
Urban/White Nile	Dummy = 1 if residence is Eddwame
Khartoum	Dummy = 1 if residence is Khartoum

Table (2): Means and Standard Deviations for all Women Age 15 or more with at least one child And By Region and Age Group

Variable	All	Rural	Urban	15-24	25-34	35-49	50+
Endogenous Household							
Children Ever Born	5.64	5.84	5.15	2.25	4.00	6.87	7.92
	(3.17)	(3.19)	(3.07)	(1.52)	(2.14)	(2.82)	(2.93)
Child Mortality	.102	.113	.073	.033	.086	.106	.160
	(.164)	(.167)	(.153)	(.114)	(.166)	(.156)	(.183)
Exogenous Household							
Woman's Age	37.8	37.2	39.1	21.9	29.0	40.8	56.4
	(11.6)	(11.9)	(10.9)	(1.85)	(2.64)	(4.42)	(6.49)
Wife's Education:							
Primary	.212	.223	.187	.298	.212	.236	.109
	(.409)	(.416)	(.390)	(.458)	(.409)	(.424)	(.313)
Secondary	.184	.109	.362	.303	.286	.131	.046
	(.387)	(.312)	(.481)	(.461)	(.452)	(.338)	(.211)
Tertiary	.037	.011	.098	.016	.081	.024	.000
	(.188)	(.104)	(.294)	(.126)	(.273)	(.153)	(.000)
Husband's Education:							
Primary	.239	.238	.241	.218	.231	.258	.226
	(.427)	(.426)	(.428)	(.414)	(.422)	(.438)	(.419)
Secondary	.218	.169	.336	.409	.287	.167	.089
	(.413)	(.375)	(.473)	(.493)	(.453)	(.374)	(.286)
Tertiary	.104	.047	.241	.053	.148	.108	.049
	(.306)	(.212)	(.428)	(.225)	(.356)	(.311)	(.218)
Log(Income/adult)	5.15	4.96	5.59	5.41	5.51	5.09	4.45
	(1.08)	(1.05)	(1.04)	(.922)	(1.05)	(1.03)	(1.01)
Exogenous Community							
Hospital Beds*10⁻²	.514	.280	1.07	.406	.526	.525	.536
	(.487)	(.297)	(.387)	(.438)	(.504)	(.482)	(.491)
Blue Nile Health Project	.367	.521		.436	.357	.363	.348
	(.482)	(.499)		(.497)	(.479)	(.481)	(.477)
Regions:							
Rural/Gezira Main	.400	.482		.383	.329	.342	.326
	(.473)	(.500)		(.487)	(.470)	(.475)	(.469)
Rural/Gezira Extension	.049	.069		.074	.056	.042	.033
	(.215)	(.254)		(.263)	(.231)	(.201)	(.179)
Rural/Eastern Gezira	.074	.104		.133	.092	.063	.027
	(.261)	(.306)		(.340)	(.289)	(.244)	(.161)
Rural/Blue Nile	.115	.163		.106	.120	.112	.120
	(.319)	(.370)		(.309)	(.326)	(.315)	(.325)
Rural/Kordofan	.128	.181		.122	.116	.130	.146
	(.333)	(.385)		(.328)	(.321)	(.336)	(.354)
Urban/Gezira	.070		.237	.027	.054	.084	.093
	(.255)		(.426)	(.161)	(.227)	(.278)	(.291)
Urban/Blue Nile	.074		.251	.074	.071	.063	.103
	(.262)		(.434)	(.263)	(.258)	(.244)	(.304)

Urban/White Nile	.051		.173	.021	.043	.063	.056
	(.220)		(.379)	(.144)	(.203)	(.244)	(.231)
Khartoum	.099		.338	.058	.116	.099	.096
	(.299)		(.473)	(.235)	(.321)	(.299)	(.295)
Sample Size	1684	1187	497	188	532	663	301

Table (3): OLS Estimates of Fertility for All Married Women Age 15 or more
with at least one child and by Region

	All		Rural		Urban	
Covariate	(1)	(2)	(1)	(2)	(1)	(2)
Woman's Age						
[15-19]						
20-24	1.194(2.10)[a]	1.150(2.00)[a]	1.252(2.00)[a]	1.182(1.89)[b]	0.015(0.01)	0.329(0.21)
25-29	2.457(4.34)[a]	2.410(4.28)[a]	2.524(4.10)[a]	2.461(3.99)[a]	1.181(0.76)	1.412(0.91)
30-34	3.366(5.94)[a]	3.370(5.99)[a]	3.500(5.65)[a]	3.427(5.55)[a]	2.000(1.28)	2.331(1.50)[c]
35-39	4.674(8.27)[a]	4.685(8.32)[a]	5.000(8.10)[a]	4.918(7.96)[a]	2.955(1.89)[b]	3.250(2.10)[a]
40-44	5.678(9.90)[a]	5.654(9.88)[a]	6.183(9.80)[a]	6.000(9.56)[a]	3.595(2.28)[a]	3.920(2.50)[a]
45-49	5.789(10.1)[a]	5.746(10.0)[a]	6.146(9.71)[a]	5.987(9.48)[a]	4.100(2.58)[a]	4.349(2.77)[a]
50+	5.951(10.5)[a]	5.920(10.4)[a]	6.116(9.80)[a]	5.922(9.47)[a]	4.587(2.90)[a]	4.962(3.16)[a]
Wife's Education						
Primary	-0.117(-0.69)	-0.245(-1.44)[c]	-0.107(-0.53)	-0.217(1.10)	-0.277(-0.91)	-0.350(-1.15)
Secondary	-1.440(-6.69)[a]	-1.388(-6.35)[a]	-1.100(-3.67)[a]	-1.187(-3.99)[a]	-1.646(-4.95)[a]	-1.557(-4.71)[a]
Tertiary	-1.980(-5.32)[a]	-1.720(-4.56)[a]	-2.133(-3.00)[a]	-2.210(-3.13)[a]	-1.816(-3.78)[a]	-1.615(-3.37)[a]
Husband's Education						
Primary	-0.176(-1.11)	-0.274(-1.70)[b]	-0.224(-1.17)	-0.332(-1.73)[b]	-0.096(-0.31)	-0.131(-0.42)
Secondary	-0.352(-1.78)[b]	-0.410(-2.00)[a]	-0.389(-1.56)[c]	-0.540(-2.16)[a]	-0.347(-0.98)	-0.249(-0.71)
Tertiary	-0.672(-2.56)[a]	-0.523(-1.94)[b]	-0.076(-0.19)	-0.231(-0.60)	-0.953(-2.37)[a]	-0.641(-1.58)[c]
Log(Income/adult)	-0.148(-2.40)[a]	-0.190(-2.95)[a]	-0.077(-1.00)	-0.155(-1.98)[a]	-0.221(-1.99)[a]	-0.212(-1.83)[b]
Child Mortality	0.963(2.64)[a]	1.136(3.12)[a]	1.144(2.63)[a]	1.355(3.10)[a]	0.433(0.65)	0.442(0.67)
Regions						
Rural/Gezira Main		1.020(4.43)[a]		0.869(4.00)[a]		
Rural/Gezira Ext.		1.085(3.18)[a]		0.968(3.12)[a]		
Rural/East. Gezira		1.087(3.62)[a]		0.939(3.39)[a]		
Rural/Blue Nile		0.600(2.11)[a]		0.489(2.10)[a]		
[Rural/Kordofan]		0.125(0.43)				
Urban/Gezira		0.763(2.61)[a]				0.738(2.54)[a]
Urban/Blue Nile		0.917(3.24)[a]				0.797(2.92)[a]
Urban/White Nile		1.052(3.31)[a]				1.031(3.38)[a]
[Khartoum]						
Intercept	2.700(4.19)[a]	2.179(3.10)[a]	2.079(2.92)[a]	1.990(2.79)[a]	4.648(2.70)[a]	3.593(2.00)[a]
R[2]	0.47	0.47	0.45	0.46	0.52	0.53
F	98.3	67.4	64.8	52.9	34.9	30.6
Joint F-test:						
Wife's Age	106.	96.3	79.8	72.8	21.8	22.9
Wife's Education	20.7	15.9	6.79	7.36	9.93	8.37
Husband's Educ.	2.25	1.85	1.02	1.87	2.48	0.98
Regions		5.44		5.00		4.82
Hausman Test:						

Log(income/adults)	-2.64	-1.05	-3.67	-1.29	-1.19	0.10
Child mortality	-1.28	-0.97	-0.86	-0.96	-3.60	3.38
Sample Size	1684	1684	1187	1187	497	497

[   ] Reference category.

Figure in parenthesis are t-statistics.

[a] Coefficient statistically significant at 5% significance level.

[b] Coefficient statistically significant at 10% significance level.

[c] Coefficient statistically significant at 20% significance level.

Table (4): OLS Estimate of Child Mortality for All Married Women Age 15 or more
with at least one child and by Region

	All		Rural		Urban	
Covariate	(1)	(2)	(1)	(2)	(1)	(2)
Woman's Age						
[15-24]						
25-29	0.052(3.46)^a	0.053(3.60)^a	0.050(2.90)^a	0.051(2.96)^a	0.058(1.83)^b	0.058(1.81)^b
30-34	0.064(4.27)^a	0.064(4.27)^a	0.058(3.27)^a	0.056(3.18)^a	0.074(2.43)^a	0.074(2.40)^a
35-39	0.057(3.82)^a	0.057(3.78)^a	0.050(2.83)^a	0.048(2.71)^a	0.066(2.17)^a	0.064(2.10)^a
40-44	0.068(4.16)^a	0.071(4.35)^a	0.071(3.61)^a	0.072(3.71)^a	0.058(1.80)^b	0.059(1.79)^b
45-49	0.069(4.16)^a	0.073(4.34)^a	0.073(3.62)^a	0.073(3.64)^a	0.062(1.91)^b	0.064(1.95)^b
50+	0.100(6.34)^a	0.103(6.46)^a	0.098(5.15)^a	0.099(5.19)^a	0.100(3.37)^a	0.100(3.38)^a
Wife's Education						
Primary	-0.019(-1.65)^c	-0.019(-1.68)^b	-0.020(-1.46)^c	-0.024(-1.74)^b	-0.014(-0.67)	-0.013(-0.64)
Secondary	-0.016(-1.10)	-0.017(-1.13)	-0.033(-1.65)^c	-0.035(-1.75)^b	0.001(0.05)	-0.001(-0.02)
Tertiary	-0.027(-1.10)	-0.031(-1.22)	-0.065(-1.37)^c	-0.067(-1.41)^c	-0.011(-0.32)	-0.010(-0.33)
Husband's						
Education						
Primary	-0.025(-2.33)^a	-0.018(-1.67)^b	-0.022(-1.73)^b	-0.016(-1.24)	-0.016(-0.77)	-0.015(-0.71)
Secondary	-0.039(-2.87)^a	-0.033(-2.46)^a	-0.037(-2.22)^a	-0.033(-1.95)^b	-0.036(-1.50)^c	-0.036(-1.47)^c
Tertiary	-0.061(-3.38)^a	-0.059(-3.28)^a	-0.043(-1.66)^b	-0.037(-1.44)^c	-0.077(-2.76)^a	-0.077(-2.76)^a
Log(Income/adult)	-0.009(-2.20)^a	-0.008(-1.80)^b	-0.011(-2.12)^a	-0.009(-1.76)^b	-0.005(-0.70)	-0.004(-0.47)
Exogenous						
Community						
Hospital Beds*10^{-2}	-0.028(-2.78)^a	-0.037(-1.74)^b	-0.044(-2.18)^a	-0.034(-1.55)^c	-0.004(-0.21)	0.009(0.36)
B.N.Health Project	-0.016(-2.20)^a	-0.037(-1.06)	-0.009(-0.77)	-0.036(-1.03)		
Regions						
Rural/Gezira Main		-0.001(-0.03)		-0.014(-0.35)		
Rural/Gezira Ext.		0.007(0.16)		-0.006(-0.22)		
Rural/East. Gezira		-0.037(-1.12)		-0.050(-2.59)^a		
Rural/Blue Nile		-0.055(-1.52)^c		-0.069(-4.40)^a		
[Rural/Kordofan]		0.014(0.38)				
Urban/Gezira		-0.029(-1.03)				0.019(0.78)
Urban/Blue Nile		-0.018(-0.83)				0.006(0.35)
[Urban/White Nile]		-0.040(-1.48)^c				
[Khartoum]						
Intercept	0.137(5.69)^a	0.150(3.34)^a	0.150(5.14)^a	0.175(5.88)^a	0.077(1.53)^c	0.048(0.75)
R^2	0.10	0.13	0.11	0.13	0.08	0.08
F	14.2	10.5	10.2	9.30	3.17	2.80
Joint F-test:						
Wife's Age	6.841	7.12	4.67	4.80	2.10	2.10
Wife's Education	1.03	1.13	1.39	1.66	0.28	0.25
Husband's Educ.	4.47	3.81	2.10	1.49	2.84	2.87

Programs	5.152	2.10	4.58	1.73		
Regions		3.28		5.32		0.30
Hausman Test:						
Log(income/adults)	2.57	2.00	3.21	2.69	0.75	0.32
Sample Size	1684	1684	1187	1187	497	497

[ ] Reference Category.
Figure in parenthesis are t-statistics.
[a] Coefficient statistically significant at 5% significance level.
[b] Coefficient statistically significant at 10% significance level.
[c] Coefficient statistically significant at 20% significance level.

Table (5): TSLS Estimate of Child Mortality and Fertility for All and Rural Married Women
Age 15 or more, with at least one child

	Child mortality		Fertility	
Covariate	All	Rural	All	Rural
Woman's Age:				
20-24			$1.110(1.76)^b$	$1.125(1.60)^c$
25-29	$0.057(3.70)^a$	$0.053(2.83)^a$	$2.010(2.68)^a$	$2.038(2.47)^a$
30-34	$0.065(4.18)^a$	$0.051(2.64)^a$	$2.900(3.62)^a$	$2.966(3.48)^a$
35-39	$0.058(3.73)^a$	$0.042(2.18)^a$	$4.262(5.56)^a$	$4.517(5.57)^a$
40-44	$0.058(3.15)^a$	$0.035(1.36)^c$	$5.139(6.11)^a$	$5.450(5.77)^a$
45-49	$0.047(2.14)^a$	$0.016(0.50)$	$5.225(6.17)^a$	$5.415(5.72)^a$
50+	$0.068(2.78)a$	$0.034(1.00)$	$5.190(5.10)^a$	$5.155(4.64)^a$
Wife's Education				
Primary	$-0.017(-1.39)^c$	$-0.023(-1.56)^c$	$-0.094(-0.37)$	$-0.011(-0.03)$
Secondary	$-0.004(-0.27)$	$-0.027(-1.22)$	$-1.250(-4.32)^a$	$-0.884(-1.80)^b$
Tertiary	$-0.043(-0.44)$	$-0.027(-0.50)$	$-1.480(-2.96)^a$	$-1.655(-1.61)^c$
Husband's Education				
Primary	$-0.005(-0.37)$	$0.012((0.67)$	$-0.146(-0.63)$	$-0.210(-0.81)$
Secondary	$-0.020(-1.29)^c$	$-0.010(-0.49)$	$-0.171(-0.48)$	$-0.282(-0.68)$
Tertiary	$-0.043(-2.11)^a$	$-0.004(-0.13)$	$-0.112(-0.20)$	$0.045(0.08)$
Log(Income/adult)	$-0.052^*(-2.26)^a$	$-0.085^*(-2.72)^a$	$-0.139(-1.50)^c$	$-0.089(-0.75)$
Child Mortality			$8.020^{**}(1.00)$	$8.880^{**}(0.98)$
Exogenous Community				
Hospital Beds*10^{-2}	$-0.034(-1.55)^c$	$-0.031(-1.30)^c$		
B.N.Health Project	$-0.037(-1.04)$	$-0.035(-0.93)$		
Regions				
Rural/Gezira Main	$-0.013(-0.29)$	$0.033(0.72)$	$1.010(3.98)^a$	$1.349(2.17)^a$
Rural/Gezira Exten.	$-0.019(-0.42)$	$0.016(0.49)$	$0.828(1.72)^b$	$1.195(2.71)^a$
Rural/East. Gezira	$-0.051(-1.47)^c$	$-0.010(-0.30)$	$1.030(3.05)^a$	$1.386(2.25)^a$
Rural/Blue Nile	$-0.089(-2.12)^a$	$-0.059(-3.37)^a$	$0.610(1.94)^b$	$1.019(1.49)^c$
[Rural/Kordofan]	$-0.025(-0.58)$		$-0.352(-0.55)$	
Urban/Gezira	$-0.054(-1.71)^b$		$0.725(2.23)^a$	
Urban/Blue Nile	$-0.016(-0.71)$		$0.910(2.91)^a$	
Urban/White Nile	$-0.032(-1.12)$		$1.127(3.12)^a$	

[Khartoum]

Intercept	$0.395(2.93)^a$	$0.528(3.60)^a$	$1.566(1.44)^c$	$0.723(0.41)$
R^2	0.12	0.12	0.43	0.40
F	9.96	8.12	55.1	41.8
Joint F-test:				
Wife's Age	3.85	1.86	30.4	24.3
Wife's Education	0.73	0.92	10.6	2.82
Husband's Educ.	1.73	0.56	0.21	0.45
Programs	1.75	1.28		
Regions	2.76	3.83	3.68	2.76
Sample Size	1684	1187	1684	1187

[ ]: Reference Category.

Figures in parentheses are t-statistics.

[*] Variable treated as endogenous and instrumented as reported in the Appendix, Table (B3).

[**] This is assumed endogenous. The predicted mortality is estimated by instrumenting on the exogenous program service as reported in Table (4), specification (2).

[a] Coefficient statistically significant at 5% significance level.

[b] Coefficient statistically significant at 10% significance level.

[c] Coefficient statistically significant at 20% significance level.

Appendix A: Selection of Sample

In the rural areas the selection of households proceeded in a multi-stage sampling process, using the administrative structure in the agricultural schemes as a sampling frame. In Gezira and Managil five groups were chosen (four in Main Gezira and one in Managil Extension). Each group consists of a total population of more than 150 thousand. Then a representative block is selected with probability proportional to population size. The villages in each block were then stratified according to the level of development as indicated by the presence of services with special emphasis on education. Thus three strata are defined according to whether all services are available in the village (primary school, junior school, health centers, midwife, and deep bore wells); some of the services available and none are available. In the final stage a representative village is selected from each strata. Thus fifteen villages were selected from Gezira. Similar procedure is followed in the other schemes, Rahad and Suki, but because these are relatively small, all groups in these schemes are included. In the final stage a sample of households was selected randomly from each village using household names which are available at rural or district council.

In the urban areas two-stage sampling procedure was followed. In the first stage residential areas are grouped into three strata based on the three residential locations: first class area, second class and third class and a representative group is selected. In the second stage household are selected at random from that group. In city planning the residential class is taken to reflect the level of income but this is not necessarily true because some rich residents of the third group are often observed. Some bias, therefore, might arise as a result in selection of households.

Appendix Table (B1): OLS Estimate of Fertility for Married Women with at least one child by Age Group

Covariate	15-24	25-34	35-49	50+
Woman's Age:	0.256(4.28)^a	0.225(7.53)^a	0.117(4.85)^a	-0.001(-0.26)
Wife's Education				
Primary	-0.096(-0.32)	-0.134(-0.57)	-0.023(-0.10)	-0.377(-0.64)
Secondary	-0.446(-1.29)^c	-1.456(-5.20)^a	-1.363(-3.21)^a	-1.383(-1.53)^c
Tertiary	-0.862(-0.90)	-2.171(-5.35)^a	-1.110(-1.42)^c	
Husband's Education				
Primary	-0.174(-0.55)	-0.413(-1.76)^b	-0.307(-1.11)	-0.217(-0.48)
Secondary	-0.556(-1.70)^b	-0.468(-1.72)^b	-0.448(-1.22)	-0.238(-0.36)
Tertiary	-0.600(-1.02)	-0.373(-1.06)	-0.838(-1.80)^b	0.504(0.53)
Log(Income/adult)	0.062(0.49)	0.244(2.87)^a	-0.372(-3.05)^a	-0.595(-3.41)^a
Child mortality	3.542(3.72)^a	1.752(3.60)^a	0.783(1.19)	0.710(0.78)
Regions				
Rural/Gezira Main	-0.118(-0.25)	0.829(2.78)^a	0.876(2.03)^a	2.231(3.38)^a
Rural/Gezira Exten.	-0.031(-0.05)	1.123(2.56)^a	1.528(2.39)^a	1.189(1.10)
Rural/East. Gezira	0.125(0.23)	0.782(2.10)^a	1.718(3.00)^a	0.394(0.33)
Rural/Blue Nile	-0.156(-0.27)	1.231(3.20)^a	0.591(1.13)	0.310(0.40)
Rural/Kordofan	-0.283(-0.49)	0.598(1.52)^c	0.554(1.05)	-0.589(-0.75)
Urban/Gezira	0.643(0.81)	1.073(2.57)^a	0.410(0.82)	1.572(2.00)^a
Urban/Blue Nile	-0.255(-0.44)	0.746(1.98)^a	0.610(1.17)	2.100(2.70)^a
Urban/White Nile	-0.347(-0.41)	0.818(1.86)^b	0.720(1.32)^c	2.868(3.24)^a
[Khartoum]				
Intercept	-3.231(-1.99)^a	-3.910(-3.56)^a	3.644(2.54)^a	9.755(5.32)^a
R^2	0.23	0.34	0.23	0.17
F	2.94	15.9	11.4	3.53

Joint F-test:				
Wife's Education	0.79	13.9	4.04	1.19
Husband's Educ.	1.08	1.34	1.14	0.28
Regions	0.33	1.86	1.77	5.47
Sample Size	188	532	663	301

[ ] Reference Category.
Figure in parenthesis are t-statistics.
[a] Coefficient statistically significant at 5% significance level.
[b] Coefficient statistically significant at 10% significance level.
[c] Coefficient statistically significant at 20% significance level.

Appendix Table (B2) OLS Estimates of Fertility and Child Mortality for All Married Women Age 15 or more with at least one child, and by Region

	All		Rural		Urban	
Covariate	Fertility	Mortality	Fertility	Mortality	Fertility	Mortality
Woman's Age[1]:						
20-24	1.150(1.99)[a]		1.199(1.90)[b]		0.013(0.01)	
25-29	2.465(4.35)[a]	0.051(3.42)[a]	2.531(4.10)[a]	0.048(2.77)[a]	1.210(0.77)	0.058(1.85)[b]
30-34	3.384(5.97)[a]	0.061(4.10)[a]	3.520(5.66)[a]	0.054(3.03)[a]	2.040(1.31)[c]	0.075(2.44)[a]
35-39	4.685(8.27)[a]	0.053(3.58)[a]	5.000(8.10)[a]	0.044(2.49)[a]	2.982(1.91)[b]	0.067(2.19)[a]
40-44	5.696(9.91)[a]	0.061(3.75)[a]	6.210(9.81)[a]	0.061(3.15)[a]	3.620(2.30)[a]	0.059(1.79)[b]
45-49	5.810(10.1)[a]	0.061(3.71)[a]	6.170(9.73)[a]	0.062(3.13)[a]	4.104(2.60)[a]	0.063(1.91)[b]
50+	6.000(10.6)[a]	0.089(5.81)[a]	6.170(9.86)[a]	0.085(4.59)[a]	4.631(2.94)[a]	0.104(3.36)[a]
Wife's Education						
Primary	-0.141(-0.84)	-0.026(-2.28)[a]	-0.141(-0.70)	-0.031(-2.30)[a]	-0.283(-0.93)	-0.014(-0.67)
Secondary	-1.465(-6.80)[a]	-0.026(-1.81)[b]	-1.134(-3.85)[a]	-0.047(-2.40)[a]	-1.645(-4.95)[a]	0.001(0.04)
Tertiary	-2.020(-5.42)[a]	-0.042(-1.67)[b]	-2.224(-3.14)[a]	-0.080(-1.70)[b]	-1.821(-3.79)[a]	-0.012(-0.35)
Husband's Education						
Primary	-0.205(-1.29)[c]	-0.029(-2.80)[a]	-0.255(-1.34)[c]	-0.026(-2.07)[a]	-0.103(-0.33)	-0.017(-0.77)
Secondary	-0.398(-2.00)[a]	-0.046(-3.51)[a]	-0.440(-1.77)[b]	-0.045(-2.70)[a]	-0.363(-1.03)	-0.037(-1.52)[c]
Tertiary	-0.740(-2.82)[a]	-0.071(-4.01)[a]	-0.130(-0.34)	-0.047(-1.88)[b]	-0.987(-2.48)[a]	-0.078(-2.87)[a]
Log(Income/adult)	-0.160(-2.59)[a]	-0.011(-2.88)[a]	-0.092(-1.21)	-0.013(-2.63)[a]	-0.224(-2.02)[a]	-0.006(-0.74)
Intercept	2.845(4.49)[a]	0.143(5.99)[a]	2.310(3.26)[a]	0.158(5.42)[a]	4.682(2.72)[a]	0.075(1.53)[c]
R^2	.47	.11	.44	.11	.51	.08
F	104.	15.5	68.57	10.9	37.42	3.41
Joint F-test:						
Wife's Age	109.	6.00	82.21	3.72	22.39	2.09
Wife's Education	21.1	2.17	7.279	2.93	9.912	0.27
Husband's Educ.	2.78	6.54	1.262	2.92	2.700	3.12
Sample Size	1684	1684	1187	1187	497	497

1. The age reference category for fertility and mortality is 15-19 and 15-24, respectively. Figure in parentheses are t-statistics.

a Coefficient statistically significant at 5% significance level.
b Coefficient statistically significant at 10% significance level.
c Coefficient statistically significant at 20% significance level.

Appendix Table (B3) OLS Estimate of Log of Household Expenditure per Adult
For Women Age 15 or more with at least One Child

Covariate	All	Rural
Woman's Age:		
25-29	$0.130(1.53)^c$	$0.077(0.79)$
30-34	$0.128(1.39)^c$	$0.054(0.51)$
35-39	$0.166(1.66)^b$	$0.093(0.80)$
40-44	$-0.089(-0.80)$	$-0.257(-1.96)^b$
45-49	$-0.338(-2.84)^a$	$-0.476(-3.43)^a$
50+	$-0.444(-3.75)^a$	$-0.464(-3.35)^a$
Wife's Education		
Primary	$0.080(1.26)$	$0.041(0.54)$
Secondary	$0.251(3.06)^a$	$0.126(1.15)$
Tertiary	$0.381(2.70)^a$	$0.484(1.86)^b$
Husband's Age	$-0.013(-1.00)$	$-0.013(-0.94)$
Husband's Age Square$*10^{-2}$	$-0.000(-0.00)$	$-0.001(-0.05)$
Husband's Education		
Primary	$0.211(3.43)^a$	$0.258(3.56)^a$
Secondary	$0.210(2.70)^a$	$0.190(2.02)^a$
Tertiary	$0.263(2.59)^a$	$0.300(2.10)^a$
Ownership of Assets		
Commercial Vehicle	$0.178(3.29)^a$	$0.156(1.87)^b$
Shop	$0.200(3.44)^a$	$0.210(2.83)^a$
Production Enterprise, Farm Machinery	$0.174(1.91)^b$	$0.227(1.67)^b$
Regions		
Rural/Gezira Main	$-0.305(-3.46)^a$	$0.645(8.35)^a$
Rural/Gezira Exten.	$-0.636(-4.90)^a$	$0.292(2.55)^a$
Rural/East. Gezira	$-0.381(-3.32)^a$	$0.550(5.45)^a$
Rural/Blue Nile	$-0.786(-7.27)^a$	$0.140(1.61)^c$
[Rural/Kordofan]	$-0.930(-8.54)^a$	

Urban/Gezira	-0.591(-5.38)[a]	
Urban/Blue Nile	0.012(0.11)	
Urban/White Nile	0.131(1.10)	
[Khartoum]		
Intercept	5.950(18.9)[a]	5.133(15.6)[a]
R^2	0.38	0.33
F	40.8	26.9
Joint F-test:		
Wife Age	11.6	8.32
Wife Education	3.88	1.33
Husband Educ.	4.64	4.58
Regions	20.0	22.1
Sample Size	1684	1187

[ ] Reference Category.

Figure in parenthesis are t-statistics.

[a] Coefficient statistically significant at 5% significance level.

[b] Coefficient statistically significant at 10% significance level.

[c] Coefficient statistically significant at 20% significance level.

Appendix Table (B4): Interaction between Parents Education and Health Programs in Child Mortality Function

Covariate[1]	All	Rural
Wife's Education		
Primary	-0.041(-1.87)[b]	-0.040(-1.67)[b]
Secondary	-0.015(-0.45)	-0.010(-0.21)
Tertiary	-0.064(-0.85)	-0.011(-0.10)
Husband's Education		
Primary	-0.034(-1.88)[b]	-0.031(-1.62)[c]
Secondary	-0.054(-1.96)[b]	-0.041(-1.30)[c]
Tertiary	-0.090(-2.07)[a]	-0.120(-2.07)[a]
Programs		
Hospital Beds	-0.067(-2.56)[a]	-0.078(-2.28)[a]
B.N.Health Project	-0.043(-1.22)	-0.041(-1.12)
Mother's Education*Hospital		
Primary	0.036(1.30)[c]	0.076(1.40)[c]
Secondary	0.025(0.77)	0.079(1.12)
Tertiary	0.057(0.97)	0.057(0.19)
Mother's Education*B.N. Project		
Primary	-0.001(-0.03)	-0.021(-0.61)
Secondary	-0.043(-1.40)[c]	-0.075(-1.41)[c]
Tertiary	-0.043(-0.62)	-0.087(-0.43)
Father's Education*Hospital		
Primary	0.029(1.10)	0.043(0.80)
Secondary	0.028(0.86)	-0.024(-0.37)
Tertiary	0.016(0.40)	-0.023(-0.26)
Father's Education*B.N.Project		
Primary	0.016(0.73)	0.010(0.26)
Secondary	0.017(0.62)	0.031(0.76)
Tertiary	0.072(1.74)[b]	0.122(1.74)[b]
R^2	0.13	0.14

F	7.28	5.94
Joint F-test:		
Wife Education	1.31	0.97
Husband Educ.	2.43	2.10
Programs	3.90	3.40
Sample Size	1684	1187

[1] In addition to the reported variables the regression included the age dummies, the regional dummies and income.

Figure in parenthesis are t-statistics.

[a] Coefficient statistically significant at 5% significance level.

[b] Coefficient statistically significant at 10% significance level.

[c] Coefficient statistically significant at 20% significance level.

Chapter Two
Female Labor Market Participation
I. Introduction

Female labor force participation and female labor supply in developed countries has been treated in a number of studies (Smith, 1980). For developing countries, Boserup, (1970) documented women's participation in the labor force and contribution to development. In these countries the bulk of women's work takes place in non-market activities in the home or the informal sector. The contribution of women to modern sector activities has been recent, but is increasing with the expansion of the market economy and advances in women's educational attainment. It is imperative, therefore, to understand the factors that lead to decisions by women to enter the labor market and how their labor supply responds to market wage earnings, income and other variables. Of particular importance are studies in developing countries that examine the impact of education on women's decisions to participate in market activities. In labor supply studies, education is found to affect the probability of female market participation positively. Following the human capital approach, some studies used education, together with such variables as years of experience and age, to derive an imputed wage that is used in the labor supply function. Others included both wages and education, and also found a significant influence (see Section 3).

This chapter looks at female labor supply, emphasizing the importance of human capital to explain the trend of increasing participation of females in market activities. An important stylized fact that has emerged from research in labor supply in developed countries is that labor force participation has gradually, but perceptibly, declined for men as a whole, whereas female labor force participation has risen substantially over time (Killingsworth, 1983; Deaton and Muelbauer, 1980). It has been argued that the observed trend in male labour force participation and supply is explainable in terms of dominance of the negative income effect that resulted from improvements in men's wages and earnings over time. In contrast, a positive and significant substitution effect of females' wages that dominates a small and initially negligible income effect is taken to explain the observed increase in females' labor force participation.

Generally in developing countries a rising trend in market participation of females has been observed. The available data for Sudan suggest that female labor force participation in urban areas of Sudan increased between 1983 and 1993. As Table A1 in Appendix A shows, the refined activity rate for females in urban areas was higher in 1993 than in 1983, increasing from 12.1% to 14.4%. Male labor force participation rates, on the other hand, declined during the period 1983-1993.

Table A2 presents the age-specific activity rates for females in urban areas. As evident from the table, women's participation rates increase with age but start to decline after women reach a certain age. In 1983 the maximum activity rate of 18.5% occurred at age group 25-29. The census of 1993 gives a maximum 23.2% at age group 30-34. Thus, participation at young age groups declined between the two censuses. This is attributed to the enrolment of more children in school, and for longer periods of time, than in 1983. The rise in the maximum activity rate in 1993 and its occurrence at the older age groups compared with 1983 may be explained in terms of demographic changes as reflected in rising age at marriage. This in turn would lead to an increasing tendency by women to stay longer in the active labor force before they marry and withdraw into home production activity.

No systematic study of female labor supply has been undertaken to elucidate the factors responsible for the observed trends in female market participation. [1] In particular, no attempts have been made to study empirically the various socioeconomic factors that influence female labor supply as evoked by the economic model of utility maximization and labor-leisure choice. With the rising trend in women's education and market participation and change in family formation in Sudan in the last decades, the issue deserves in-depth treatment.

This research applies recent econometric techniques to available micro level data on female labor supply to shed light on some of the regularities and facts revealed by labor surveys in Sudan. The importance of the changing role of women and their involvement in labor market activities, and thus the potential importance of intra-family substitution effects, as well as the change in overall educational attainment, will be emphasized. The study continues my examination of the impact of education on development, (Maglad, 1993, 1994)[2] by extending the analysis to labor supply decisions. The data set generated in the earlier project is used in this research, supplemented by recent micro level data collected by the Ministry of Manpower in 1991 (see Section 4).

The remaining sections of this chapter proceed as follows: In Section II the theoretical framework is elaborated, while Section III examines the empirical specifications and some conceptual issues and the estimation methodology. Section IV presents the empirical results and Section V concludes the discussion with a summary and implications.

2. Theoretical Framework

The simple neoclassical static model of labor supply without uncertainty assumes that the individual maximizes his utility function, U, defined as the amount of market (i.e., consumer) goods, C, which are assumed to be a composite commodity, and hours of leisure L, consumed per period, subject to income and time constraints; that is:

$$\text{Max}_{1,c} \ U(C,L) \tag{1}$$

Where the income constraint is defined as:

$$PC = WH + V \tag{2}$$

P is the price of a unit of C, W is the fixed price of an hour of L (wage per hour) and V is other non-labor income, such as property income. So spending on market goods must equal income from work plus other income. Total available time T may be allocated between leisure L and work H. Thus,

$$H = T - L \tag{3}$$

The optimum occurs where the marginal rate of substitution of consumption for leisure, $M = (\delta u/\delta L) / (\delta u/\delta C)$, is equated to the ratio of prices, W/P, which is the real wage rate. Thus:

$$M = (\delta u/\delta L) / (\delta u/\delta C) = M(C,L) = W/P \tag{4}$$

By solving equations 2 and 4 the optimal quantities of labor supply, H, and consumption goods, C are derived as functions of prices (P,W) and property income, V. Thus $H = H(W, V, P)$. Writing $w = W/P$ and $v = V/P$, the labor supply for a given individual may be written as $H = H(w, v)$, and indicates the absence of money illusion.

The model as outlined above deals with the labor supply decisions of the individual. To extend the model to labor supply decisions by the household, particularly the two-person household (wife and husband), the wage offer available to the other spouse must be added to the list of variables determining the reduced-form equation of market labor hours, if both spouses engage in some market activity (Mincer, 1962; Kosters, 1966; Heckman, 1974; Schultz, 1980; Killingsworth, 1983).

The impact of a change in i's labor supply to a unit change in j's wage is written as the sum of the substitution and income effect:

$$\delta H_i \:/\: \delta W_j = S_{wj} \,(H_i) + H_j(\delta H_i \:/\: \delta V)$$

Where S_{wj} is the substitution effect, and refers to the effect of a wage change with property income adjusted so as to keep utility constant – that is the effect of an income compensated wage change – and the second term on the right-hand side is the income effect of the change W_j on H_i.

The predictions of the theoretical model are the following:

1. *Negativity of the income compensated own-wage substitution effect:* A rise in the wage rate leads to a decrease in the demand for leisure and hence a rise in labor supply, so the income compensated own-wage elasticity of labor supply is positive:

$S_{wi} \,(H_i) \; W_i \:/\: H_i > 0.$

2. *Symmetry:* Income compensated cross-substitution effects $S_{wi}\,(H_j)$ and Swj (H_i) must be equal. Also, the income compensated cross-substitution effect of one spouse's wage offer on the other spouse's labor supply may be negative or positive. This depends on whether the leisure time of one spouse is a substitute or complement for leisure time of the other spouse in the household.

3. Negative income elasticity: $(\delta H / \delta V)(V/H) < 0$. An increase in an individual's income as a result of wage increases leads to demand for more leisure, and consequently to lower labor supply than before the rise in the wage rate.

3. Econometric Specification and Estimation

Specification:

Labor supply functions derived using the theoretical framework in Section II will not provide a complete model for empirical estimation for two reasons. First, the function derived assumes that the individual works, i.e., an interior solution to the maximization problem facing the individual. Second, data used for estimation pertain to different individuals with different tastes for work, that is individuals differ not only in terms of the observable variables (i.e. w, v) but also in terms of the non-observable (which are represented by a random error term, ϵ).

Regarding the first problem, one should observe that an individual would work only if the market wage rate, w, exceeds a reservation wage, w*. The latter is given by the value of marginal rate of substitution when L=1, that is when no market labor hours are offered, and it represents the marginal value of time in non-market activities. Thus, assuming freedom of choosing hours of work and absence of fixed cost of work, it is assumed that an individual's labor supply behavior is determined by two relationships: (1) a market wage offer or a market demand function, w, and (2) a shadow value of time or reservation wage, w*, or the individual's labor supply function:

$$w = f(X, \ \epsilon 1) \tag{5}$$

$$w^* = g(Z, H \ \epsilon 2)$$
(6)

X and Z are vectors of possibly overlapping exogenous and endogenous variables that determine the market wage offer and the individual's labor supply function. H is hours of work, $\epsilon 1$ and $\epsilon 2$ are randomly distributed stochastic terms that reflect non- observable factors such as abilities, taste for work, errors in measurement and purely stochastic variability. The market demand function in Equation 5 is assumed to be independent of hours worked (Heckman, 1974). The individual will work if and only if $w >$ $w*$ and the hours of work of any individual who works are defined by the relations $w = w*$, and hence may be obtained by solving this relation for H.

Assuming, for example, that the functional forms for equations 5 and 6 are linear, one can write the demand and supply functions, respectively, as:

$$w = a_0 + \alpha 1\, X_i + \epsilon 1_i \tag{7}$$

$$w*_i = \beta_0 1 + \beta_1 Z_i + \beta_2\, H_I + \epsilon 2_i$$
(8)

Where i refers to individual i and α's and β's parameters to be estimated. Solving for the hours of work equation yields:

$$H_i = 1/\beta_2\, (w_i - \beta_0 - \beta_1 Z_i) - (1/\beta_2)\, (\epsilon 2i) \tag{9}$$

$$H_i = 1/\beta_2\, (w_i - \beta_0 - \beta_1 Z_i) + v_i$$
(9')

$$H_i > 0 \text{ if and only if } \epsilon 2i < - (w_i - \beta_0 - \beta_1 Z_i)$$
(10)

$$H_i = 0 \text{ if and only if } \epsilon 2_{i>} - (w_i - \beta_0 - \beta_1 Z_i) \tag{11}$$

As equations 9', 10 and 11 reveal, the model gives an account of both participation (that is the decision to work or not to work) and hours of work.

It also shows that the same parameters, observable variables and unobservable random error affect both kinds of decisions.

Estimation:

OLS estimates of a function like that depicted in Equation 9' will suffer from selectivity bias since the error term in samples used for estimating the labor supply parameters will not be a zero-error random variable. The problem arises because the error term that determines the sample selection rule would be correlated with the error term of the supply function. This occurs whenever the selection rule is endogenous to labor supply, e.g., selecting on the basis of income or employment, as in use of the sample of working individuals.

As noted above, labor supply means both participation and hours of work. The analysis begins by considering the female's participation decision, that is the decision of being, or not being, employed. In this case the dependent variable will take the value of one or zero depending on whether a woman works or not. If one makes the assumption that v_i is a normally distributed random variable, a probit equation, whose parameters may be estimated by the method of maximum likelihood, can be estimated.

Hours of work are accounted for in the analysis, through a Tobin likelihood function. By estimating probit or Tobin probit, one can get estimates of the parameters that govern the labor supply and hence income and wage elasticities. It is also possible to analyze the determinants of the decision to work or not to work, since the estimates can be used to calculate the probability that a given female, with given values of Z and W, will or will not work. If only workers are used in the sample to estimate the labor supply parameters, then consistent estimates can be obtained by correcting for selectivity bias using selection bias corrected regression (Heckman, 1976, 1979, 1980).

One problem with this methodology is that the wage variable is not available for all N observations. To counter this, we assume that the market wage function (Equation 7) estimated for the workers only sample can be used as a basis for imputing wage rates to those with and without observed wages. The imputed wage rate derived using the OLS estimates of the parameters of the function in Equation 7 is:

$$\hat{W} = \alpha_0 + \alpha_1 X_i \tag{12}$$

Which can be used in Equation 9 in place of w? Now the problem is that OLS estimates of Equation 7 will suffer from selectivity bias as the estimation is based on the workers only sample. The practice is to correct for the sample selectivity bias by using the Heckman two-stage procedure (Heckman, 1980). This procedure involves estimating a participation function in the first stage, either a probit or logit depending on the assumptions made regarding the error term, to derive an inverse Mills ratio. The ratio so derived is then used in the second stage OLS estimation as a regressor to correct for specification bias that results from excluding the sample of non-workers from the regression. While the estimates yielded by the Heckman method are consistent, they are not asymptotically efficient. For this reason, the preferred alternative is the full information maximum likelihood (FIMIL) approach.

Generally, the early empirical studies of labor supply found that income compensated own-wage elasticity is positive for males and lies between 0.000 and 0.360; that for females is found significantly positive and ranges between 0.100 and 2.000. As for the income elasticity, for males it is usually weak and negative, lying between 0.000 and –0.160, but in some studies not significantly different from zero. For females, it is generally negative and much greater in absolute value than the male elasticity, ranging between – 0.100 and –0.2000 (Killingsworth, 1983).

Also, gross (uncompensated) wage elasticities are indicated in some studies to be positive for women and negative for men. The range of estimates for the uncompensated own-wage elasticity for women is larger than the range of estimates for men: between about 0.200 and 0.900 (0.00 to –0.40 for men) in most aggregative cross-section and micro level cross-section studies of female labor supply (Killingsworth, 1983). In later studies, which took account of sample selectivity bias and endogeneity of the wage rate, female gross wage elasticity is usually at least 0.60 and often yields estimates in excess of 2.0. When education is used as a determining variable, its effect is found to be positive (Schultz, 1980; Malathy, 1989).

Empirical specification of the wage and labor supply function

The wage function that I apply to the data is the well-known human capital earnings function (Mincer, 1962; Mincer and Polachek, 1974), which assumes that the proportionate change in wage earnings is determined by a number of wage variables. These include years of schooling, S, years of post-schooling experience, EX, and its quadratic EXSQ. An error term ϵ_{1i} representing the effect of unobserved factors (e.g., motivation, innate ability, etc.) on wages, is assumed to be normally distributed with a zero mean and constant variance. Thus the wage function is specified as:

$$\ln W_i = \alpha_0 + \alpha_1 S_i + \alpha_2 EX_i + \alpha_3 EXSQ_i + \epsilon_{1i}$$

(7')

Where $\ln W_i$ is the natural logarithm of the female's hourly wage rate and *EX* is approximated by age minus age of entry into the school system (seven years) minus years of schooling completed. It is argued that this "potential" experience variable is inadequate to use as a measure of past experience to explain change in female market productivity, since for women the length and continuity of market experience varies a great deal. Nonetheless, once schooling is determined, potential experience is not subject to individual control and may thus be independent of the error term in the right-hand side. On the other hand, if entry and exit from the labor market are assumed to be individual control and may thus be independent of the error term in the right-hand side. On the other hand, if entry and exit from the labor market are assumed to be individual choice variables, this variable cannot be considered as exogenous and will be simultaneously determined with the wages, and hence correlated with the unobserved abilities and preferences. A test of the exogeneity of this variable will be carried out.

The estimating equation of the labor supply function is:

$$H_i \quad = \quad \beta_0 \; + \; \beta_1 \; \hat{W}_i \; + \; \beta_2 \; \hat{W}_h \; + \; \beta_3 \; V \; + \; \beta_4 \; Z_i \; + \; \epsilon 2_i$$
(9'')

Where H_i is the annual hours worked by the wife, $\hat{W}_i$ and $\hat{W}_h$ are the wife's and husband's predicted hourly market wage rates, V is the household assets in the last five years, Z_i is a vector describing some demographic characteristics like the wife's age, squared term in age, and children in two age groups: pre-school and school age.

The use of an instrumental wage also controls for the average hourly earnings measurement error and purges the wage variable from the correlation with the error term that arises from endogeneity of the actual wage rate. Similarly, the inclusion of children among the right-hand variables would give rise to simultaneity problems, since fertility and labor supply decisions are thought to be endogenously determined. This will be dealt with in two ways: (1) by estimating the function without this variable and (2) by testing for the exogeneity assumption.

4. Empirical analysis

Data:

Official statistics pertaining to the labor force, its size, socioeconomic characteristics, participation, earnings and migration have been collected through the Ministry of Manpower (MOM) (formerly Ministry of Labor). Some information on labor size, participation, employment status, distribution by occupation and industry is also part of the various population censuses carried out by the Central Bureau of Statistics in 1973, 1983 and

1993. The Ministry of Manpower carried out two surveys on labor and migration, one in 1990 another in 1994, and a third is being completed this year (1996). None of these surveys meet all the data requirements for the analysis proposed in this study.

For this reason the main data set I use to analyze the determinants of female labor supply in Sudan come from a demographic survey I conducted in 1990/91 with the financial support of the Rockefeller Foundation. The survey sample contains information on female participation and labor supply and a variety of socioeconomic variables relevant to the proposed analysis. (For a description of this sample see chapter 1). The official data of the Ministry of Manpower will be used whenever possible during the process of analysis.

The 1990/91 survey covered both rural and urban areas in the central and western states of Sudan. The primary unit in the survey was the household, which was chosen by a multi-stage stratified random sampling. Information was collected separately for women in the household, with emphasis on the wife and other married women. Thus, data on female marital status, education attainment, number of children, market participation, wages, husband's income, household assets etc., are available.

Only the sub-sample of women resident in urban areas is used for the analysis of labor supply in this study. There were 627 households, and this sample forms the basis of the analysis of female labor supply in urban areas. Out of this total, 128 (18%) participated in market work. About 90% were employees, the majority of whom worked in professional and clerical occupations, a pattern also observed in the 1993 Population Census. Because of the small size of the sample all observations are used, including the few self-employed in service activities.

Some measurement problems of labor supply, hours of work, and the wage variable and its imputation will need to be addressed. I use the hourly wage rate for the wage variable, which is defined as weekly earnings divided by usual hours worked last week. For the labor supply I use annual hours worked last year, which is defined as the product of the usual average hours worked last week and the weeks worked last year.

The means and standard deviations of the variables used in the empirical analysis are provided in Table 1. It is seen from the table that a female labor force participation of 0.18 is observed for the sample used in the study. For the purpose of this study participation is equated with employment. This is unlike the definitions of Table A1 and Table A2 in Appendix A, where participation means being in the labor force, and hence includes the unemployed among the participants. In Table A2, a participation rate of 19.6% is noted for women in their forties in 1993 (which is the mean sample value).

Table 1: Variable definitions, means and standard deviations (SD)

Variable	Working Women		All Women	
	Mean	SD	Mean	SD
Labor force participation			0.18	0.39
Annual market hours	1,456	684.3	273.9	641.6
Wife's imputed hourly wage	3.08	0.86	2.66	0.76
Explanatory				
Years of schooling	8.78	5.78	5.91	5.55
Experience	22.12	13.03	27.25	16.06
Experience square	658.1	737.9	1,000	1,006
No. of children < 6 years	0.68	0.81	0.69	0.92
No. of children 6-15 years	1.08	1.25	1.06	1.29
Husband's imputed hourly wage	18.35	9.95	16.6	10.25
Asset $(x10^{-4})$	7.985	55.71	12.83	90.16
Age	37.9	9.07	40.2	12.3
Age square	1,518	777.3	1,765	1,094
Males 16 years & over	1.80	1.74	2.56	1.98
Females 16 years & over	2.82	2.58	2.81	2.22
Household structure	0.22	0.41	0.17	0.37
Life-time migration dummy: Non-migrant = 1, else = 0	0.67	0.47	0.61	0.49

Sample size	128	693

The Wage Function

Table 2 presents estimates of the Mincerian wage function. Each column shows two regressions, one without the experience square term and the other including the quadratic of experience. Other specifications, which included the square of education and interaction terms of education and experience, were tried and estimated (not reported) but didn't give better estimates than those in Table 2. Column 1 gives the traditional estimates of the equation, which uses the sample of working women to estimate the parameters of the wage function through OLS. The regression corrected for sample selection bias is presented in column 2 and column 3, where in the former Heckman two-stage procedure is followed and in the latter full information maximum likelihood (FIML) is used. FIML is preferred since it provides asymptotically efficient estimators.

Adopting the sample selection correction procedure increases the estimated returns on schooling for women from an average of 3%, obtained through traditional regression, to 8%; the coefficient on the selectivity termλ, indicates that there is some evidence that the sample of wage earning women is not a random sample of the population with regard to their wage rate.

Table 2: Estimates of the wage equation (t values in parentheses)
Dependent variable: In hourly wage

Explanatory variable	(1) Traditional regression		(2) Traditional regression Corrected censoring [a]		(3) Maximum likelihood Estimates [a]	
Education	0.033	0.029	0.082	0.077	0.070	0.056
	(1.81)	(1.58)	(2.41)	(1.50)	(1.94)	(1.07)
Experience	0.003	-0.018	0.012	0.007	0.011	-0.008
	(0.37)	(-0.88)	(1.22)	(0.17)	(1.15)	(-0.19)
Exp. Square		0.037		0.007		0.030
$(\times 10^{-2})$		(1.11)		(0.12)		(0.50)
λ			0.639	0.579		
			(1.50)	(0.87)		
Intercept	1.425	1.689	-0.148	0.026	0.225	0.804
	(4.32)	(4.15)	(-0.16)	(0.01)	(0.22)	(0.46)
R^2	0.04	0.04	0.04	0.03		
Rho					0.507	0.328
					(1.14)	(0.43)
Log Likelihood					-451.1	-450.9
N		128		128		128

Note: [a]Estimates of the reduced form participation equation used for sample selection correction is given in column 1 of Table 3.

The estimates of the wage function confirm the positive effect of schooling on earnings, which is reported in the literature. The estimates of the experience coefficients, however, are not precise and are statistically insignificant in all regressions. It is often argued that experience cannot be treated as an exogenous variable, since the number and periods of stay in the market place could be affected by a woman's own choice and hence the variable would be correlated with the error term and the estimated coefficients would be biased. It is to be noted that the variable used in the analysis is more a measure of potential experience than of actual experience. In fact, when the variable is replaced by an instrumental variable estimate, the impact of education is obscured and no change is observed in the estimates of experience term. [2] It is therefore decided to use the maximum likelihood estimates of the wage equation, where experience enters in a linear form (first regression in column 3, Table 2), for predictions of the wife's wage equation. [3]

Labor Force Participation Decision:

Table 3 provides estimates of the labor force participation equation. These are the maximum likelihood estimates of parameters of the probit model. The latter estimates are preferred to the OLS estimates since it is established that MLL provides asymptotically consistent and efficient estimates.

Three regressions are provided in the table. The first regression does not include the numbers of pre-school and school age children, while in the second regression these variables are introduced in the function. Since fertility and labor supply decisions are simultaneously determined, these variables would be endogenous and hence correlation with the error term would give biased and inconsistent estimates of the parameters. In order to test for endogeneity of the children variables in the labor supply equations, instrumental variables estimates are used in place of actual values and test of endogeneity is applied. [4]

The problem arises in finding appropriate instruments to identify the children equations, since most of the variables that enter the labor supply equations can be thought of as determinants of fertility. In want of such variables, I have assumed that adult members of the household, household structure, and lifetime migration status could be treated as identifying variables. The structure of household is a dummy variable used to reflect whether the household is made up of an extended family or a single unit (nuclear) family. It takes the value of one for an extended household and zero otherwise. It is suggested that household structure plays a role in decisions regarding work or number of children. This is because it is easier to find substitutes for the mother's time at home when other adults, particularly females, live in the same household and can provide the required child care where these inputs could not be easily purchased in the market (Wong and Levine, 1992). [5]

The instrumental variable regressions of the suggested children equations are shown in Appendix B, Table B1. Form Table B1 it is seen that of the identifying variables, only adult males and adult females are significantly and negatively related to young children. There are two possible interpretations for the negative related to young children. There are two possible interpretations for the negative relationship between these variables and small children. One is that married women at the start of their marriage, and hence with a few small children, may be living in extended households, with large number of adults. The other is that the adults may include the daughters and sons of the woman, as those women with a large number of children at old age are less likely to still have a large number of young children. The labor force participation regression including the instrumental variables of small and older children is shown in column 3 of Table 3.

The estimates in Table 3 indicate the positive and significant influence of education on the woman's decision to enter the labor force. Moreover, in the first and second column of Table 3, post-schooling experience is positively associated with labor force participation of the woman. The negative quadratic experience term indicates that participation is concave on experience; that is, the probability of being in labor market activities is higher the longer the woman spends in market activity, but declines after she reaches a certain age. Also, the coefficient of the head's instrumental wage indicates that a woman's participation in the labor market is reduced significantly as the head's predicted wage rises. [6] Household assets have a negative effect on the woman's entry into labor market activities but is not statistically significant.

Regarding the effect of young children on market participation by women, the results in column 2 of the table, when actual values of children are entered, indicate a negative but insignificant impact, and no change in the estimated parameters of the other variables is noticeable. However, when the instrumental variables of children are introduced in column 3, presence of pre-school children and a woman's decision to participate in the market is noted.

But the introduction of instrumental value of children affects the magnitude and significance of other estimated parameters in the model. Most notable, the coefficients of experience are now imprecisely estimated. So, it appears that there is some interaction between the wife's labor force experience variables and the number of children in the household. This might be because post-schooling experience is a residual of age over years spent at school, and these post-schooling years overlap in time spent in having children, childcare and market activity. In fact, as it will be seen later, when a woman's age is introduced in labor supply function together with predicted children the effect of the former on labor supply is obscured (this is discussed further in the next section).

Moreover, with predicted children in the regression, in column 3 of Table 3, both the magnitude and significance of household assets and the husband's instrumental wage are increased. Not that the test of endogeneity, at the bottom of Table 3, implies that children cannot be treated as exogenous variables in participation equation, at least when experience and not the woman's age is introduced in the function.

The Labor Supply Function:

Estimates of the labor supply function are presented in Tables 4.1 and 4.2. Table 4.1 provides two sets of estimates:

- Column 1 shows the estimates of a standard Tobit, in which instrumental wage corrected for selectivity bias is used (for both woman and head) and introduced as a regressor in the supply of hours equation.
- Column 2 introduces the instrumental wage corrected for sample censoring into the structural participation and hours worked decisions.

These are estimated separately, in the first case for all women and in the second case for working women only. The selectivity bias in the conditional hours equation is corrected by using FIML approach.

Each column of Table 4.1 supplies two regressions. The first regression excludes actual values of children, whereas the second one introduces these variables. A test of endogeneity of children is given in Table 4.2, where the instrumental variables of children are introduced for both standard Tobit and generalized Tobit.

Table 3: Regression on female labor force participation (t values in parentheses)

Explanatory variable	(1)	(2)	(3)
Education	0.128	0.124	0.071
	(6.060)	(5.78)	(1.91)
Experience	0.087	0.088	-0.042
	(4.48)	(4.15)	(-0.76)
Experience square $(x10^{-2})$	-0.121	-0.128	0.010
	(-4.02)	(-3.88)	(0.17)
Husband's wage [a]	-0.019	-0.019	-0.023
	(-2.64)	(2.67)	(-3.05)
Assets $(x10^{-4})$	-0.001	-0.001	-0.002
	(-0.86)	(-0.84)	(-1.67)
Children < 6		-0.082	-1.420
		(-1.05)	(-2.28)
Children 6-15		-0.029	0.737
		(-0.57)	(2.38)
Constant	-2.59	-2.412	0.206
	(-7.49)	(6.34)	(0.15)
Log likelihood	-331.6	-331.6	-295.8
X^2	64.63	66.35	71.55
Endogeneity test:			
X^2			6.393
N	693	693	693

Note: [a] predicted wage.

The results of the standard Tobit in column 1 of Table 4.1 indicate that hours of work are positively and significantly affected by the woman's own wage. The response of the woman to the head's wage is negative and significant. The household's non-labor income, though it reduces market hours provided by the woman, is not statistically significant. Market labor hours of the woman are related to her age in a positive and declining manner reflecting the life cycle effects. A negative, but not important, impact of children's presence on the hours a woman provides is noted. In fact, none of the estimated coefficients of the regressions offered in Table 4a are changed appreciably in magnitude or significance by the introduction of children, when the latter are assumed exogenous.

The generalized Tobit method estimates are shown in column 2 of Table 4.1. The participation decision estimates are presented first, where the dependent variable is a dummy variable taking the value of one if a woman is working, and zero if she is not working. Since OLS are inappropriate for estimation, a probit is estimated. The exercise reveals that the woman's decision to enter the labor market is positively and significantly affected by her predicted wage rate. Moreover, a woman is less likely to enter labor market activities if her husband's wage rate increases, and this wage effect is statistically significant. Non employment income of the household negatively affects the decision to participate in market activities, but is not statistically significant. The effects of age show that younger women are more likely than older women to participate in market activities. The peak in the estimated participation rate occurs at about age 40.

Column 2 of Table 4.1 also shows estimates of the conditional hours (hours worked by women working). These estimates are corrected for sample selection bias, but as the results indicate, sample selectively bias appears not to be an important problem in the estimation of the hours of work function in this instance. With the exception of the head's wage rate, which is only weakly related to hours supply, none of the other variables seem to have an impact on labor supply decisions. This suggests that the

61

income effect of the head's earnings plays an important part in hours work supplied by the woman. Again, no further insight is gained by the inclusion of actual value of children in the estimated labor supply functions.

Table 4.1: Estimates of labor supply equations (asymptotic t values in parentheses)

Without instrumental variables of children

Explanatory Variable	(1) Standard Tobit		(2) Generalized Tobit			
	Hours		Part	$Hours^b$	Part	$Hours^b$
Female's wage [a]	1386	1386	0.6394	76.80	0.6306	89.17
	(6.60)	(6.50)	6.70	(0.24)	(6.56)	(0.28)
Husband's wage [c]	-49.89	-49.56	0.0203	-15.93	-0.0201	-16.40
	(-3.10)	(-3.09)	(2.70)	(-1.26)	(-2.69)	(-1.24)
Assets x 10^{-4}	-2.502	-2.417	-0.001	-1.249	-0.001	-1.284
	(-1.00)	(-0.97)	(-0.85)	(0.14)	(0.81)	(-0.14)
Female's age	345.2	360.4	0.1829	-29.39	0.1899	-37.81
	(4.01)	(3.84)	(4.36)	(-.035)	(4.17)	(-.42)
Fem. age square (x10^{-2})	-426.1	-439.9	-0.2206	42.18	-0.2324	52.73
	(-4.08)	(-3.97)	(-4.43)	(-0.42)	(-4.31)	(0.48)
Children < 6		-100.9		-0.0560		24.66
		(-0.62)		(-0.70)		(0.25)
Children 6-15		-80.15		-0.0394		30.89
		(-0.76)		(-0.77)		(0.50)
Constant	11513	-11511	-5.832	2344	-5.810	2398
	(-5.89)	(-5.50)	(-6.44)	(0.77)	(-5.97)	(0.78)
Log likelihood	-1323	-1323	-293.3	-1289	292.6	1288
Rho				-0.3812		-0.3582
				(-0.49)		(-0.45)
N	693		693	128	693	128

a. Predicted wage, obtained by using maximum likelihood estimates of the wage coefficients shown in Table 2, column 3.

b. The reduced form participation equations used as the basis for selection into the sample are the probit equations of column 1 and column 2 of Table 3.
c. Predicted wage.

The standard Tobit framework is based on the assumption that the participation and hours of work decisions arise from a single framework. If this is correct, the sign and statistical significance of the related parameters should be similar. As the results in column 2 of Table 4a show, the participation decision is more responsive to the determining variables than the hours of work decision, implying that the generalized Tobit is to be preferred to the standard Tobit.

In Table 4.2 the instrumental variable estimates of children are introduced for the standard Tobit in column 1 and for the generalized Tobit in column 2; the test of exogeneity of the variables is reported at the bottom of the table. The introduction of predicted children alters the size of the parameter estimates of the standard Tobit and the generalized Tobit.

Most notably, the previous conspicuous influence of the wife's age in labor supply in the standard Tobit, and in the labor force participation decision in the generalized Tobit, it is no longer apparent. Probably this arises because of the strong correlation between the wife's age and the number of children (Table A3), which apparently has been carried over in the predicted variables. In this formulation, the size and significance of the husband's wage and household assets are increased. The presence of young children appears to discourage participation and reduce the number of hours a woman offers in the market. The presence of older children, who are likely to be in school and thus release her of day-time activities at home, encourages her participation in market work.

Table 4.2: Estimates of labor supply equations (asymptotic t values in parentheses)

With instrumental variables of children

Variable	Standard Tobit Hours	Generalized Tobit Part	Hours
Female's wage [a]	1465	0.6825	475.1
	(6.03)	(6.10)	(1.40)
Husband's wage [c]	-56.86	-0.0234	-33.66
	(-3.32)	(-2.89)	(-2.37)
Assets x 10^{-4}	-4.310	-0.001	-2.420
	(-1.42)	(-1.23)	(-0.26)
Female's age	64.02	0.013	-129.0
	(0.17)	(0.07)	(-0.61)
Fem. age square (x10^{-2})	-38.71	-0.0618	79.11
	(-0.11)	(-0.36)	(0.40)
Children[d] < 6	-2434	-0.9756	-1691
	(-1.10)	(-0.88)	(-1.26)
Children[d] 6-15	1197	0.5173	500.4
	(1.10)	(0.96)	(0.69)
Constant	-1383	-1.734	4231
	(-0.15)	(-0.38)	(0.87)
Log likelihood	-1323	-292.8	-1284
			-0.6880
Rho			(-1.77)
Endogeneity text χ^2	1.26	0.918	6.52
N	693	693	128

a. Predicted wage, obtained by using maximum likelihood estimates of the wage coefficients shown in Table 2, column 3.
b. The reduced form participation equations used as the basis for selection into the sample are the probit equation of column 3 of Table 3.
c. Predicted wage.
d. Instrumental variable estimates.

The effect of children, however, is not statistically significant and the test of the exogeneity of children indicates that the hypothesis that children are exogenous cannot be rejected in the standard Tobit and the participation function in column 2. In the Tobit with sample selectivity (second regression in column 2 of Table 4.2), the test rejects the exogeneity assumption of children. Moreover, there is an indication of sample selection bias in the generalized Tobit when children are endogenized. In this regression a positive and weakly significant effect of the female's predicted wage on market hours is noted, and a strong negative relationship with the husband's wage is indicated. Young children, who require home care and attendance, cause a woman to spend less time in market activities but the effect is only marginally significant.

Labor supply, uncompensated own-wage, cross wage and income elasticities are calculated at sample mean values using the estimated parameters of the alternative estimating procedures for specifications where children are excluded, as their presence did not much affect the estimates in most regressions. The elasticities are presented in Table 5. If the terms of the participation equation and hours worked equation are assumed to be independent, then the sum of the elasticity of participation and the elasticity of conditional hours worked should approximate the Tobit elasticity of the expected value locus.[7] As seen from Table 5, expected labor supply elasticities with respect to own-wage and spouse's wage are slightly larger than Tobit expected value locus elasticities, with the difference reaching 0.2. These elasticities are difficult to compare with estimates obtained for other developing countries because of differences in sample composition, coverage, variable definitions, etc. In particular, Mroz (1987) has shown, the estimated response of the variables is sensitive to choice of identifying variables and the specifications used. Nonetheless, compared with findings for India (Malathy, 1992), for example, these estimates of own-wage elasticities, are higher.

Table 5: Labor Supply Elasticity according to Alternative Estimation Procedures

Procedure	Own-wage	Husband wage	Assets
Standard Tobit[a]	2.16	-0.48	-0.019
Generalized Tobit			
1- Hours worked (H.O)	0.15	-0.21	-0.006
2- Probability of working	2.21	-0.44	-0.014
Expected labor supply (1+2)	2.36	-0.65	0.018
OLS[b]	2.71	-0.52	-0.012

a. The elasticities are with respect to the expected value locus (not the Tobit Index) and hence analogous with the OLS elasticities at the bottom of the table. Note that $\delta E (H)/\delta x_i = \beta_i \phi (\beta'x)$, where, $\phi (.)$ is the distribution function evaluated at the mean values.

b. Based on OLS estimates of hours worked using the sample of all women; these are shown in Appendix B, Table B2.

5. Summary and Concluding Remarks:

This chapter examined the economic variables determining women's decisions to enter market activities. The price and income variables were found to affect these decisions in accordance with the underlying theoretical framework of the utility maximization and leisure-labor choice. Maximum likelihood and bias-corrected regressions were used to get unbiased and consistent estimates of the participation and labor supply functions and wage function.

Regarding the wage functions, the human capital earnings function was applied to the data. It was revealed that education affects growth in the wage earnings positively and significantly. When sample selection-corrected estimates of the earning function were used, a higher average rate of return on women's education was found (8%) compared with those obtained using conventional methods, and some evidence of sample selection bias was detected. Experience as defined by number of post-schooling years was not found to affect wage growth significantly. This result may be peculiar to the sample analyzed, since data from other sources show that post-schooling experience significantly influences wage growth.

As for the labor force participation decision and labor supply, the study found that both are affected positively by predicted own wage and negatively by the spouse's predicted wage earnings. While market entry was positively and significantly correlated with a woman's years of education, and subsequently with the market wage rate, it appears that the amount of time a woman puts in labor market activities is determined largely by the earnings of her husband. The negative effect of the husband's earnings on the woman's labor supply may reflect the dominance of the income effect of the husband's wage change and also the substitutability of time of husband and wife in non-market activity. This negative effect of the husband's predicted wage on market hours appreciates in magnitude and significance when children are endogenized in the regression of conditional hours.

One striking result of the analysis is the effect of the presence of children on women's market participation and labor supply. When children are taken as exogenous, their effect is found to be small and marginally significant. Evidently, small children tend to discourage participation by a woman in market work (but this is only marginally significant), whereas older children encourage market work and their effect is definitely not significant. Since age is controlled for in the regressions, it was argued that the large and significant effect of age on market participation could also reflect the impact of children on women's market activity, since the presence of children is found to be positively linked with age. In fact, the inclusion of an instrumental variable for children gives a significant response coefficient of the latter and brings a drastic reduction in the response and significance of age on the probability of market participation.

Some further explanation for the minor effect of children's presence on market participation seems to be called for. The provision of child care and the ease of getting it could explain why children might not significantly deter a woman from market work. In the context of the traditional society within which the studied women live, I suspect that young women are more likely to be living with their extended families at the start of their marriage and can easily get help with child care from relatives. On the other hand, this result may be peculiar to the sample I studied and therefore analysis of other samples is required.

Another striking finding of this study is the strongly positive link between women's education and their market participation in urban Sudan. Obviously, the human capital investment in women through education increases their access to opportunities to work in market activities and raises their market productivity compared with home production. As the analysis has shown, a woman's wage is positively and significantly associated with her years of schooling, and the labor she supplies to the market responds positively to increases in the predicted wage offer. Also, as is found in studies of fertility and child health, an educated woman, with a higher opportunity value of time, tend to bear fewer children and to invest more in them through better education and health. Thus it would seem that intergenerational links in education of parents and their children persist. It should be noted that the impact of human capital investment on poverty and inequality are beyond the aims of this research and need to be addressed in a separate study.

Own-wage elasticities in magnitude of 2.2 to 2.4 were obtained, whereas a cross-wage elasticity of 0.65 to 0.90 is implied by the regression estimates. Though it is difficult to compare these estimates with findings of other studies, because of differing sample composition, coverage and selection, they are within the received empirical findings range. Compared with a study for urban India, for example, own-wage elasticity is higher, but as in the Indian study, the wage elasticity is higher in the generalized Tobit than in the standard Tobit estimation method.

In the sum, the findings of this study imply that investment in women's education would lead to expansion of women's involvement in market activities, as education affects directly their decision to engage in market work, and has an indirect effect by its positive impact on market wage growth. Given that own-wage elasticity for participation largely exceeds the husband's cross-wage elasticity, a general wage rise that leaves men's to women's wage ratio constant is expected to lead to an expansion in women's labor market participation in urban Sudan.

Notes

1. The household production model deals directly with the allocation of time between market and home production activities, and the implications for labor supply when treated within the household framework (Becker, 1965). More recently, family labor supply behavior has been treated in some studies (Schultz, 1990) in the context of bargaining models of family members (Manser and Brown, 1980; McElroy and Horney, 1981).

2. The study presented in Maglad (1993, 1994) was conducted with financial support from Yale University and the Rockefeller Foundation; it studied household behavior in terms of family size and investment in children.

3. The question of identifiability of an experience function arises, since most of the variables that might be suggested to influence experience also simultaneously determine labor supply. The experience equation I used included, in addition, such variables as other adult females, household structure and lifetime migration.

4. Using the Migration and Labor Survey of 1991, the following semi-logarithmic wage function is estimated by OLS:

L_n Wife's Wage = -0.113 + 0.052* Education + 0.044* Experience
$\qquad$ (-1.15)$\quad$ (8.35) $\qquad\qquad$ (6.27)
$\qquad\qquad$ -0.0005*(Experience)^2; $R^2 = 0.12$, N = 654
$\qquad\qquad$ (3.45)

Figures in parentheses are t statistics.

5. The likelihood ratio is used to test for the endogeneity of the variables. This ratio is defined as $LR = [L\ (w)/L\ (\phi)]$; $L\ (w)$ and $L\ (\phi)$ are, respectively, the likelihood values of the constrained and unconstrained models. It can be shown that -2 log (LR) is distributed as χ^2 with degrees of freedom equal to the number of constraints.

6. According to the 1993 Population Census, extended family households in urban Northern Sudan were 37.5% of total private households. Moreover, composite family households, which form a larger component that includes some relatives with/without their spouses, amount to 14.6%. Other relatives constituted 13.5% of the total population in private households in urban areas. In rural Northern Sudan extended plus composite households amounted to 49.2%. The other relatives' proportion of the total population of private households was 6.5%

(Department of Statistics, 1996). The growth in the number of extended households relative to nuclear ones in urban areas in the 1990s can be attributed to the growing number of immigrants, displaced persons and refugees after the 1980s.

7. The wage function for men is estimated using the sample of working men only, since about 9% of the men in the sample are either retired or not working. Sample selectivity bias is corrected for by using maximum likelihood estimates, and the sample selection probit equation is identified by the family's landholding, adult males, adult females, lifetime migration and household assets. Of these variables only that for adult males is statistically significant and negatively related to probability of being employed. However, the selection-corrected maximum likelihood estimate of schooling returns was not found different when the conventional OLS method was used. The sample selection corrected estimate of the wage was:

L_n Husband wage = 0.656 + 0.111 *Education + 0.058 *Experience
$\qquad\qquad\quad$ (1.50) $\qquad\quad$ (5.89) $\qquad\quad$ (3.11)
$\qquad\qquad\quad$ -0.006* (Experience) ^{2}; ρ = -0321;
(-0.99)
$\qquad$ N = 629. Figures in parentheses are the t ratios.

8. See Schultz (1980) for derivation.

References:

Abbot, M. and O.Ashenfelter. 1976. "Labor supply, commodity demand and the allocation of time". Review of Economic Studies. Vol. 43:389-411.

Ashworth, J.S. and D.T. Ulph. 1981. "Endogeneity estimating labor supply with piecewise linear budget constraints". In C.V. Brown, ed., Taxation and Labor Supply. London: Allen and Unwin.

Becker, G.S. 1965. "Theory of the Allocation of Time". Economic Journal, vol.75:493-457.

_____, 1975. Human Capital 2nd edition. New York: Columbia University Press. Birdsall,N. 1985. "Public inputs and child schooling in Brazil." Journal of Development Economics, vol. 18, pp.67-86.

Boserup, 1970. The Role of Women in Economic Development. New York: St. Martin's London: Earthscan.

Chernichovsky, D. 1985. "Socioeconomic and demographic aspects of school enrolment and attendance in rural Botswana". Economic Development and Cultural Change, no.2:319-332.

Census Office, 1995. Fourth Population Census of Sudan 1993, Final Tabulations, Sudan Northern States, vol. 2, Economic and Social Characteristics. Khartoum: Department of Statistics.

_____. 1989. Population and Housing Census of Sudan, 1983, National Report: Summary Analysis and Statistical Tables. Khartoum: Department of Statistics.

Department of Statistics. 1996. Fourth Population Census of Sudan 1993: Analytical Report. Khartoum: Department of Statistics.

Deaton and Muelbauer. 1980. Consumer Behavior. Cambridge: Cambridge University Press.

Heckman, J.J. 1974. "Shadow prices, market wages, and labor supply." Econometrica, vol. 42, no. 4: 679-694.

_____. 1976. "The common structure of statistical models of truncation, sample selection, and limited dependent variables and a simple estimator for such models". Annals of Economic and Social Measurement 5:475-92.

_____. 1979. "Sample selection bias as a specification error". Econometrica, vol. 47:153-62.

_____. 1980. "Sample selection bias as a specification error with an application to the estimation of labor supply functions". In Smith, 1980.

_____., M.R. Killingsworth and T.E. MaCurdy. 1981. "Empirical evidence on static labor supply models: A survey of recent developments". In Hornstein, Grice and Webb, ed. 1981: 75-122. The economics of the labor market. London: Her Majesty's Stationery Office.

Jamison, D.T. and M.E. Lockheed, 1987. "Participation in schooling: Determinants and learning outcomes in Nepal". Economic Development and Cultural Change, vol. 26, no. 2: 279-306.

Manser, M. Brown. 1980. "Marriage and household decision making: A bargaining Analysis". International Economic Review, vol. 21: 31-44.\

Maglad, N. 1994. "School supply, family background and gender-specific school enrolment and attainment in Sudan". Eastern Africa Social Science Research Review. Vol. X, no. 2 (June).

_____. 1993. "Socioeconomic determinants of fertility and child morality in Sudan". Discussion Paper No. 686. New Haven, CT: Economic Growth Centre, Yale University.

Mroz, T. 1987. "The sensitivity of an empirical model of married women's hours of work to economic and statistical assumptions". Econometrica, vol. 55 no. 4: 765-799.

Psacharopoulos, G. 1981. "Returns to education: An updated international comparison". Comparative Education. vol. 17: 321-41.

Schultz, T.P. 1992. "The role of education and human capital in economic development: "An empirical assessment". Discussion Paper No. 670. New Haven, CT: Economic Growth Centre, Yale University.

_____. 1980. "Estimating labor supply functions for married women". In J.P. Smith, ed., Female Labor Supply: Theory and Estimation, Princeton, N.J.: Princeton University Press.

_____. 1990. "Testing the neoclassical model of family labor supply and fertility". Journal of Human Resources, vol.25. no.4: 599-597.

Singh, R.D. 1992. "Underinvestment, low economic returns to education and schooling of rural children: Some evidence from Brazil". Economic Development and Culture Change. vol. 40. no. 3: 654-664.

Smith, J.P.1980. Female Labor Supply: Theory and Estimation. Princeton, N.J.: Princeton University Press.

Wong, R. and R.E. Levine. 1992. "The effect of household structure on women's economic activity and fertility: Evidence from recent mothers in urban Mexico". Economic Development and Cultural Change, vol. 41, no. 1:89-102.

Appendix A: Selected historical labor data for Sudan

Table A1: Refined labor force participation rates (%), by sex and mode of living in Northern Sudan, 1983-1993

Mode of living and sex	1983[a]	1993[b]
Urban:		
Females	12.1	14.4
Males	69.2	68.4
Both sex	42.5	42.4
Rural:		
Females	34.7	34.5
Males	77.9	73.0
Both sex	55.0	51.8

Sources:

[a]1983 Census: National Report, Summary Analysis and State Tables, Table 19 and 46.

[b]1993 Census: Sudan Northern States, vol.2, table EI and vol. 1, Table PI.

Table A2: Females' age-specific refined activity rates (%) in urban Northern Sudan, 1983 and 1993

Age group	1983[a]	1993[b]
10 - 14	5.18	4.37
15 - 19	8.77	8.72
20 - 24	17.93	14.70
25 - 29	18.15	21.31
30 - 34	14.87	23.18
35 - 39	13.01	19.64
40 - 44	14.00	19.56
45 - 49	13.21	18.00
50 - 54	14.25	16.29
55 - 59	13.13	13.41
60 - 64	13.98	13.57
65 +	10.34	10.4
10 +		
Not stated	9.26	-
All ages	12.1	-

Sources:
[a]1983 Census: National Report, Summary Analysis and Statistical Tables, Table 46B.
[b]1993 Census: Final Tabulations, Sudan Northern States, vol. 2, Economic and Social Characteristics, Table E1.

Appendix B: Selected Results of Model Runs

Table B1: Instrumental variable estimates of children equations
(t-value in parentheses)

Variable	Children < 6		Children 6-15	
Wife's education	-0.0125	(1.54)	0.0301	(-2.42)
Wife's age	-0.0933	(-6.28)	-0.1363	(5.98)
Wife's age square(x10^{-2})	0.0632	(3.91)	-0.1753	(-7.07)
Husband's wage	0.0062	(0.93)	0.0351	(3.43)
Husband's education	-0.0197	(-1.47)	-0.0743	(-3.61)
Husband's age	-0.0019	(-0.53)	-0.0049	(-0.91)
Asset	0.0002	(0.56)	0.0018	(3.66)
Other males	-0.0416	(-2.27)	-0.0949	(-3.38)
Other females	-0.0408	(-2.39)	-0.0553	(-2.11)
Household structure	-0.0294	(-0.33)	-0.0794	-0.58
Lifetime migrant	-0.0341	(-0.55)	-0.0599	(-0.63)
Constant	3.7977	(10.82)	-0.4465	(-0.83)
R^2	0.309		0.174	
F	29.10		14.28	
N	693		693	

Table B2: Ordinary least squares of the labor supply function
(t-value in parentheses)

Explanatory variable	Hours		Hours	
Female's wage	281.0	(7.59)	280.5	(7.51)
Husband's wage	-8.697	(-3.20)	-8.714	(-3.20)
Asset $(x10^{-4})$	-0.255	(-0.98)	-0.255	(-0.98)
Female's age	39.50	(3.60)	38.22	3.20
Female's age square x 10^{-2}	-46.66	(3.78)	-45.71	(-3.46)
Children < 6			-11.80	(-0.38)
Children 6 - 15			1.349	(0.07)
Constant	-1087.	(4.26)	-1044.	(-3.72)
R^2	0.08		0.08	
F	14.4		10.3	
N	693		693	

Chapter Three

Wage Earnings and the Private Returns to Education

1. Introduction:

This chapter examines the factors influencing variation of wage earnings in Sudan. A number of theories were advanced in labor market literature to explain wage differences and differential of wages among individuals with similar attributes. These range, from the classical theory of equalizing wage differences attributed to Adam Smith (1910), the segmented labor market theories (Leontaridi, 1998), emphasizing the fragmentation of non-competing labor markets which is caused by institutional and social factors, to the neoclassical human capital theory (Mincer, 1974, 1980; Schultz, 1960, 1961; Becker, 1962,1964), which emphasize differences in ability and skills acquired by the individual through education and training as the explanation of observed wage differences.

In Adam Smith view wage differential between individuals may exist as compensation for agreeable and disagreeableness of employment and to compensate for the cost of learning business. Adam Smith also recognized immobility of workers between the different occupations due to institutional regulation and laws of apprenticeship and trade as a factor that impedes competition to equalize wage differentials.

On the other hand, the institutional school emphasizes the importance of internal labor markets (ILM) created within firms and dictated by the modern organization structure and technology used by firms, as an important explanation for pay differences and recruitment policies. Implicit in the ILM theory is the importance of training and skills acquired as underlying pay differences within firms. Two important factors which are identified for the emergence of the ILMs are the specificity of training on the part of employees which entails increased training, recruitment and screening costs, and the need to build stable and loyal personnel (Doeringer and Piore, 1971). Thus herein its demand factors by the firm for specific labor quality and skills that are driven by firm's desire to minimize costs (of labor turnover) that lie behind the pay differences within firms.

In this chapter the human capital framework is used to explain differences in wage earnings using data from the National Baseline Household Survey 2009. It focuses on the determining factors specified in the human capital model, which emphasizes education and training as important among the factors explaining wage inequalities.

The general education system of Sudan has changed twice in the last two decades. Initially composed of three levels: primary, intermediate and secondary, with duration of four years each, the system was modified in 1971 with the duration of primary level extended to six years and the intermediate and secondary level reduced to three years each, to become the general secondary (junior secondary) and high secondary, respectively. In 1991 a second change took place with the primary and junior level being merged into an eight years basic education level and the secondary level remaining at three years. In addition, the age of admittance to the primary school level (first grade primary level) was changed from age seven to age six.

With these changes in the education system it is difficult to get a meaningful comparison over time of changes in enrollment rates for a given level of education. However, the 2009 NBHS indicates that net enrollment rate in primary school (persons ages 6-13) is 67%, with a higher rate of 69% for males compared to 64% for females. Only about a fifth (22%) of secondary school age population (14-16) are enrolled in secondary schools, with a higher rate for females (23%) compared to male (21%). Literacy rates for population 10 years and above is 66% with higher rates for males at 75% compared to 56% for females. Literacy rates are also higher in urban areas at 82% compared to rural areas, where just over half the population is literate (56%). The rates in urban areas are 89% and 75% and in rural areas 66% and 45%, for males and females, respectively.

Similarly, the tertiary level of education has undergone a landmark change in 1989. The number of public universities increased from 4 universities to 26 in 2005, with almost one university in each of the then 26 states. This expansion was a response of the Government to replace an elitist higher education, where only about 6% of those who used to sit for the School Certificate Examination were able to find a place in a higher institution of education, with one which provides an equal opportunity for admission to any student eligible for such level. It is also in line with a declared policy to achieve balanced development through enhancing the local capacities and skills of the population, promoting growth and thereby laying the foundation for political and social stability.

In parallel with the public expansion in higher education private universities and colleges also increased, from only 3 in 1989 to 35 in 2001 (MHESR, 2001) with the majority being established in Khartoum (77%), where both income and demand are higher compared with other regions. As a result of these developments, the number of admissions to higher education witnessed an unprecedented increase, with the number of students increasing from 6080 in 1987/1988 to 48170 in 1999/2000. Admission in 1999/2000 represented 32.2% of the total number of students successfully completing the Secondary School Examination in that year.

Despite these tremendous expansion in quantity, the expenditure on education remained at low levels, with education expenditure representing an average of only 5.3% of Government budget and less than 1% of GDP between 2000- 2005. The impact of these meager allocations to education would undoubtedly be deterioration on the quality of services offered, with consequent implications on the productivity and gains from the received education. Thus, one of the questions with which this study will be concerned is whether the expansionary policies in education have led to declined rates of returns from education.

The remaining sections are organized as follows: in section 2 the theoretical background and the empirical specifications and associated estimation issues will be described. Section 3 deals with sample and the data used in the empirical investigation. In section 4 and 5 the empirical findings are presented and final conclusions are presented in section 6.

2. Theoretical and Empirical Framework:

2.1. Theory and Empirical issues:

In the human capital model for analyzing the wage earnings differential schooling represents an investment. Since the individual incurs costs by engaging in schooling, both directly in the form of costs of tuitions, books, transports and other related expenses, and indirectly by foregoing labor market earnings while at school in the form of wages, these costs of investment are expected to be repaid by the future flow of enhanced earnings, and the rate of return is the one which discounts the future flow of benefits from schooling to equate it to the present value of private costs of investment. Thus, on the supply side, in order to induce an individual to forgo earnings and other related costs of education future life time earnings must be sufficiently higher to compensate her for the incurred costs. On the demand side, schooling must increase the marginal productivity of the more educated workers compared to those with less education in order to command higher wages for their increased education level. Viewed this way wage differentials reflect the differences in individuals' human capital.

Under some simple assumptions the human capital framework can be illustrated. Suppose that costs of schooling consist only of foregone earnings and that the rate of return to education r is the same for all levels of schooling. Then the present discounted value of future earnings, obtained after investing in s schooling years and working for n years after finishing school, must equal the discounted value of forgone earnings, representing the cost of schooling, that is

$$\int_{s}^{s+n} e^{-rt} Y_s \, dt = \int_{0}^{s} e^{-rt} Y_0 \, dt \qquad (1)$$

Integrating we get:

$$Y_s \, e^{-rs} (1 - e^{-rn})/r = Y0 \, (1 - e^{-rn})/r \qquad (2)$$

From (2) we get

$$Y_s = Y_0 \, e^{rs} \qquad (3)$$

Where Y_0 represents forgone earnings while at school, and is assumed to be fixed over the years of schooling, s. Appending a multiplicative disturbance term e^u and taking logarithm of both sides of equation 3 we get

$$\text{Ln } Y_s = \ln Y_0 + rs + u \qquad (4)$$

In the work of Mincer (1974, 1976), equation (4) became the basis for regressing the logarithm of earnings on years of schooling as an explanation of earnings, and as a theory of the distribution of earnings. This interpretation is based on a number of assumptions. In addition to assuming that non-pecuniary benefits of different jobs are irrelevant and that individuals face and can borrow at the same interest rate, and that labor markets are competitive, it is assumed that individuals perceive future earnings correctly and that higher ability individuals get no extra benefits from education but get multiplicatively higher earnings.

If equation 4 is fitted by least square to data on schooling and the logarithm of earnings, the estimated slope coefficient provides estimates of r that can be interpreted as the average private rate of return or the opportunity cost of schooling for a representative individual[1].

Formal schooling is not the only means by which skills are acquired. Skills can be acquired through on-the-job training ranging from formal training and apprenticeship to informal means of learning by doing. The wage and labor supply implications of on-the-job training human capital accumulation has been considered by Becker (1962, 1964) and Mincer (1962,1974), among others. In order to capture variations of earnings with age or market experience, Mincer (1962, 1974) added a quadratic in post schooling market experience, approximated by age –schooling (A-s) ;

$$\ln w = \alpha + \beta_o s + \beta_1 (A\text{-}s) + \beta_2 (A\text{-}s)^2 + \mu \qquad (5)$$

Many problems arise in the empirical estimation of returns to schooling (Schultz, 1992). Firstly, returns to schooling may be estimated imprecisely because of inadequate specification of the wage-schooling relationship. Estimation bias may arise because of difficulty in specifying student ability, family background, and school quality. These problems may influence returns to schooling of men and women differently. If years of schooling are correlated with the individual ability then the estimated coefficient on years of schooling will be biased upward. But due to the difficulties of obtaining measures of ability and the complex relationship between ability, education and earnings, no conclusive evidence seems to have been reached regarding the size and direction of the bias (Willis, 1986; Grilliches, 1970, 1977).

Secondly, problems arise because market productivity is observed for a portion of the total population, which reports wages needed for the estimation of returns to education. The selection into the sample of wage-earners gives rise to selectivity bias, since this selection is most probably not independent of schooling-wage-productivity relationship.

In such cases, the problems of sample selection involve explaining both labor supply behavior and wage determination. This is important for comparisons of returns to education of men and women, since men and women participation in market activities and labor supply behavior are different.

If education produces a wealth effect that induces a reduction of the labor supply of the more educated and an increase in non-market production and leisure, then an underestimation of returns to schooling could result if annual or monthly earnings are used as a basis for comparisons. On the other hand, the price or substitution effect of education is expected to increase hours supplied. In this case comparison of annual earnings overstates private returns. Thus, the preferred dependent variable used in estimation of the earning function is the logarithm of the hourly wage rate.

A related issue is how to incorporate unemployment in the estimation of the private returns to education. This issue is particularly relevant for comparisons of returns to education of men and women, because of difference in unemployment rates among these groups, which is usually higher for women than men. If education increases the probability of employment, then adjustment of returns to education for unemployment rate should result in a rise in the former. Recent research has pointed to the importance of labor market conditions on individuals' decision regarding participation in labor market activities or continuation on further education induced by high rates of unemployment, especially among the young age groups (Clark, 2002; Pastore, 2005; Kuru et. al, 2009). One implication of this body of research is that choices regarding employment and investment in education are not independent. The question of endogeneity has been treated in the literature by using Instrumental Variables (IV). Devereux and Fan (2011) used the educational expansion in the United Kingdom as (IV) to deal with endogeneity and study the effects of education on earnings.

Another bias arises in the estimation of private returns to schooling when particular groups of workers are used as a basis for estimation of earnings relationship. In most human capital studies of returns to education, the sample used in estimation is the sample of employees, since it is easy to observe their labor earnings more directly whereas imputation of net earnings of the self-employee would require deduction of own and purchased input, a task which is surrounded by many difficulties. In developing countries, where a large portion of the labor force is in self-employed activities, estimated returns to education based on the sample of employees alone could not be taken as representing average returns to education to the whole population.

Relying on the sample of wage-earners to estimate private returns to education would also give biased estimates of the returns to the average individual in population, since non-participant in market activities might be involved in non-market productive work, which is also influenced by education. This bias may be more serious for women, who are engaging more than men in productive home work. Thus one of the main occupations of research in human capital in recent years has been an endeavor to correct for the bias that may be introduced in the analysis because the sample of wage-earners may be more (or less) productive than the average person.

The methodology for correcting the bias due to the sample selection has been to estimate both the wage function and a probability function determining the likelihood of being in market or wage employment (Heckman, 1974; 79; 80). The usual assumption in labor economics is that people undertake a market job when the net wage offer (net of tax and fixed cost of work) exceeds a reservation wage rate. The latter is determined by the individual's productivity in non-market or home activities.

The sample selection bias corrected methodology of estimating both a wage and labor participation function raises some statistical problems regarding the identification of the wage function and the choice of the identifying variables. The methodology requires existence of some exogenous variables which are highly correlated with the probability of participation in market activities but are not related to the wage function.

One of the issues with which this research will be concerned is to assess how is the correction for the sample selection-bias affect estimates of the private returns to schooling levels for men and women and how it modifies the gender differences in returns to schooling. The question of identifying variables will also be addressed in the analysis (section 2.1 below).

Finally, it should be noted that, though the basic model used in this paper is concerned with estimating private returns to education this does not underestimate the importance of non-monetary returns to education as has been uncovered in many studies in the impact of education on decisions regarding fertility and family size, health and investment on children, choice of occupations, awareness and many other spheres. Also, some recent research has gone into examining the effect of relaxing some of the underlying assumptions of the model such as the assumption of a risk-free returns to education or that an individual is risk neutral (see Harmon, 2011, for review of research advances in these issues).

2. 1. Specification and Estimation:

The wage function which we shall apply to the data from the National Household Survey 2009 is the well-known human capital earnings function developed in the preceding section. The function assumes that the proportionate change in the wage earnings is determined by a number of wage variables, including years of schooling, S, years of post-schooling experience, X, and its quadratic X^2, and an error term μ_i, representing the effect of unobserved factors (e.g. motivation, innate ability, etc.) on wages, and which is assumed to be normally distributed with a zero-mean and constant variance. Thus, the following relationship is postulated,

$$Ln\ W_i = \alpha + \beta_0 S_i + \beta_1 X_i + \beta_2 X_i^2 + \mu_i \quad (6)$$

Where i refers to the ith worker and $Ln\ W_i$ is the natural logarithm of individual's i monthly wage rate, which shall be used in the absence of hourly wage rate. If both variables were available we would have been able to compare differences in the returns to schooling that might be attributed to variation in labor due to increases in education. The more educated are expected to have lower monthly earnings as they tend to enjoy more leisure, because of the wealth effect arising from more schooling.

Experience will be approximated by age minus age of entry into the school system minus years of schooling completed [2]. It is argued that this "potential" experience variable would be an inadequate measure of past experience, since for some people they might not be attached full time to market work after completing their schooling; which is particularly true of women. However, once schooling is determined, potential experience is not endogenously determined, and hence is independent of the error term in (6). Some studies used interaction terms between schooling and experience, which I experimented with at the initial stages of estimation but turned out as insignificant and removed from the final specification.

The basic model may be refined to include different levels of schooling. If S_{ik} stands for level of schooling k by individual i then a version of equation (6) can be used that allows the estimated rate of return to vary by level of education, so that:

$$\text{Ln } w_i = a + \Sigma \ \beta_k \ S_{ik} + c \ X_i + d \ X_i^2 + \mu_i \qquad (7)$$

Where k stands for the level of education (i.e. k = primary, intermediate, secondary, and post-secondary level).

As mentioned in section 1, the relationship in (6) and (7) is observed only for a subpopulation, that is wage earners, and if this sample is observed because it is more productive than other groups in the entire population, then the selection rule that determines the sample will be endogenous to the wage productivity relationship. In this case, the error term that determines the sample selection rule would be correlated with the error term in the earnings function. OLS estimation of (6) would result in biased estimates of the schooling coefficient. Alternative methods of estimation have sought to correct for this sample selection bias by inclusion of the process generating the observation of wage earners (Heckman, 1979).

It is postulated that an individual accepts a wage earning job when the market wage offer exceeds his reservation wage, which is determined by the individual's marginal productivity at home or non-market involvement. The difference between the market wage offer and productivity in alternative non-market activities determines the probability of participating in wage employment (Heckman, 1974). This is represented by the following wage earner choice relationship,

$$W^* = \beta'Z + \varepsilon_i \qquad (8)$$

Where W^* is a latent variable reflecting an individual's occupational choice into wage employment. Z is a vector of individual, family or community characteristics that influence this choice, and ε_i is a random error term. The observed counterpart of W^* is a binary variable, W, taking the value of 1 if W^* is positive and hence the person is a wage earner and zero otherwise. ε and μ have a bivariate normal distribution with respective variances σ^2_μ and σ^2_ε, where the latter is normalized to one. The correlation coefficient between ε and μ is denoted by rho, ρ. Thus, the following probit specification is implied,

$$\text{Prob } (W = 1) = \text{Prob } (\varepsilon i > -\beta'Z) = F \ (\beta'Z) \qquad (9)$$

Where F ( ) is the cumulative density function of ε_i.

The maximum likelihood estimate of the system of equations (8) and (9) provides consistent and efficient parameter estimates. Because it is hypothesized that the variables that appear in the right hand side of (8) also influence the individual's decision to enter wage employment activities, the vector Z should include some additional variables to identify the wage function. Schultz (1990, 1991) suggested non-earned or property income. The argument is that these variables raise the shadow value of time of home or self- employment activities, and as a result reduce the probability of participating as a wage earner.

Of the other variables which are suggested as identifying variables in a woman's participation function are children, since they raise a female's productivity at home (Gronau, 1974). This is true in the short run, since over the life cycle fertility responds to labor market wage, and therefore is endogenous, or simultaneously determined with market labor supply decisions. A person's spouse market productivity could also be viewed as appropriate identifier, as it increases the value of an individual's time at non-market activities. Land ownership and household business assets are also being suggested as identifiers for the same reason.

In this analysis household non-earned or property income and land ownership are used as identifying variables. Some studies included regional shifters in the functions to take account of the effect of wage and price differences that are due to regional variation, and purge the estimated returns to schooling from the bias that might result if differences in productivity across regions are not controlled. These differences in productivity are captured in the process of regional migration from low to high-wage regions, as in migration from rural to urban areas or between regions. Estimating the participation and wage function with and without regions as determining variables would shed light on the effect of migration in the estimation of school returns.

2.3. Empirical Studies of Education's Returns and Findings:

Based on extensive reviews of studies on returns to education in developed and developing countries Psacharopoulos (1981, 1985, 1994) calculated private and social aggregate rates of return. The following findings were revealed:

(i)   Based on Mincerian wage functions' coefficients on years of schooling, the average rate of return for the world is 10.1%. The rates of return were found to vary by region, and were 13.4%, 12.4%, 9.6% and 8.2% for Sub-Saharan Africa, Latin America/Caribbean, Asia and Europe/Middle East and North Africa, respectively.

(ii)   The higher the level of schooling the lower the return to education. Thus, returns to primary schooling are higher than those for secondary level, which in turn are higher than those for higher levels (Appendix: Table A5). This finding holds in the case of private rate of return as well as the social rate of return across different world regions. The high profitability of primary education, it was argued, is attributable to its lowest cost in comparison to other levels as well as the substantial productivity differential between workers who complete primary education and those who are illiterate.

(iii)   Also the more developed the country the lower the rates of return to education; returns to education for each level decline by the country's per capita income level. This reflects the fact that the law of diminishing returns also applies to the investment in human capital formation. The empirical findings which support these facts were summarized in (Table A6 in appendix).

(iv)   In low-income countries, the private returns to higher education are twice the social returns, because public costs of education constitute a large portion of total costs. The large divergence between private and social returns in Africa implies that the education in the continent, particularly higher education, has been largely subsidized.

(v)   The findings reveal too that returns to women education are higher than those for men. But those calculated by level of education show a more mixed pattern. Table A7 in appendix exhibits this finding. Also, as girls' schooling in most low income countries started lately, the cost of public subsidies in females' education is lower compared with that on males, and because education of girls involves some additional external non-market gains, social returns to schooling of girls are expected to exceed returns from boys' schooling. Thus it is argued that public support of girls' education is recommended on both efficiency and equity grounds.

(vi)   Returns to education are believed to vary by sector of employment. In this respect, returns for the employees who work in the private/competitive sector are higher (11.2%) than for those in the public/non-competitive sector of the economy (9%). These results lend support to the hypothesis that earnings measure the productivity of workers and were thus, justifiably, used in the calculation of the returns to education.

A number of studies used the procedure of correcting for sample selection bias in estimating returns to schooling. Khandker (1989) estimated returns to schooling of Peruvian men and women. Returns to schooling of women increase with correction for sample selection bias, and returns were higher for women than men at secondary and higher schooling levels. However, an analysis of Peruvian data by King (1989), using Heckman two-stage procedure for sample selection correction, reduced the women returns to schooling at different school levels.

A study of returns to schooling in Thailand (Schultz, 1990, 1989) revealed a similar pattern, where the sample-selection correction tended to raise returns to female schooling and lower them to males. Also, an analysis of earnings of married women in the Philippines (Griffin, 1987) found that average returns to schooling of women are higher (18 percent) compared with returns obtained from estimation based only on the sample of wage earners (14 percent).

Tansel (1994) used the sample selection correction to estimate returns to schooling for Turkish wage earners by gender. The estimated correlation coefficient between the error terms of the probit wage earner and log earnings equations is found to be statistically significant for men but insignificant for women, indicating that estimating the log earnings function on a selective sample of wage earners would produce biased estimates for men. The implied ML estimates of men's rates of return that are corrected for sample selection bias are found to be somehow higher for high school and university level. As for women, the OLS estimates of the returns to education are about the same as the corresponding selectivity corrected MLE's.

Assad (1997) examined public-private wage differentials for male and female in Egypt by using a double selection framework that extends the single selection procedure developed by Heckman (1976,1979) and Lee(1976) to account for two selection rules jointly determining participation in nonagricultural wage work and sector selection (public/private). Assad's findings indicate that returns to primary education are very low in Egypt, estimated for the private sector at 2.3 % for males and for 4% for females. In the public sector estimates to primary education are 8.0% for females and 3.7% for males. Furthermore, private rates of return to education are significantly higher at the university level, which is estimated at 8.6 % for females and 8.2 for males in the public sector and at 20.6 % and 8.8% for females and males in the private sector, respectively, than at the secondary level which is 6.2 % for females and negative for males in the private sector; 7.2% for males and 7.8% for females in the private sector.

Cohen and House (1994) fitted a Mincerian function to data from a limited survey of formal sector employees in urban Khartoum to estimate returns to education. In their study, the estimated rate of return to an additional year of schooling is 9.3 per cent, which is less than that reported by Psacharopoulos for other African countries (13 %). Furthermore, they found that returns increase with levels of education. For instance, their estimated rate of return to tertiary education is 12.6 %, which is significantly higher than the estimated rate of return to primary education (4.6 %). However, one of the major drawbacks of their study is that the estimated rates of return are based on survey data limited to formal sector employees in urban Khartoum and as such not representative of the population.

Maglad (1993) (chapter 2 in this book) estimated average proportionate rates of return to education for married women based on data obtained from a limited household sample survey conducted in Central Sudan and Khartoum Province in 1990/91. Fitting a Mincerian-type function to the data of female workers, he found that the rate of return to education for females is around 3 percent. Applying the sample selection technique, the estimated returns for females increased from 3 percent to 8 percent.

A number of country-case studies for some countries in the Gulf and North Africa are provided in research undertaken by Arab Planning Institute. The country-case study of Oman (Maglad and Elhagry, 2002) revealed that an average marginal rate of return for an additional year of education is between 9% - 10%, and is consistent with the average found in other studies. On the other hand, the error-corrected maximum likelihood estimates of educational returns resulted on lower estimates for males (9% compared to 10%) and higher estimates for females (16% compared to 11%).

Wage-differentials by education of men and women are examined from African household surveys by Schultz (2003). The analysis suggested private returns in six African countries are highest at the secondary and postsecondary levels, and rates are similar for women as for men. Vijverberg (2001) estimated wage and nonfarm self-employment earning functions for Cote d'Ivoire corrected for selectivity bias based on a choice model of three regions and four employment modes. Rates of return to education in Cote d'Ivoire are high for both men and women, but men's wages exceed women's by a substantial margin for all but the most educated.

Other studies have attempted to deal with the bias in the estimated rates of return that is related to omission of unobserved variables which may be connected with productivity. One such variable is the quality of public services, specifically school quality, which tend to influence productivity which if not controlled for in estimating the earning functions result in estimated parameter of schooling that will be biased upward, since it will be capturing both the effect of school quantity and quality.

Bias in the estimated education parameters could arise also because of omission in the regression of family background, which acts through genetic and environmental factors to influence ability. If the family characteristics affect productivity and are correlated with years of schooling, their omission will bias upward estimates of return to schooling. This form of bias is treated in some studies by including proxies for school quality and family background through estimation of wage models with community fixed-effects and household fixed-effects (Behrman and Deolalikar,1988).

3. Sample and Data:

The data analyzed in this paper are from the nationwide household budget survey: National Baseline Household Survey 2009. The survey consisted of 7920 households drawn randomly by two stage sampling procedure, where an equal number of 528 households in each of the 15 states in Northern Sudan were chosen from the primary sampling units (44 units in each state). The sample comprised 48845 individuals. The field work for the survey was undertaken from 17th of May- 30th June 2009.

The sample examined in this paper is confined to 25963 individuals in the labor force, ages 15 to 64, who reported information on educational attainment, earnings and other labor market characteristics. The sample is broken in table 1 by rural-urban location and gender. The average labor force participation rate is 52%, with participation rates of 78.4% for men and 26.9% for women. Participation rates are higher in rural than urban areas, with rates of 80.5% and 28.8% for men and women in rural areas, and 74.5% and 23.1% in urban areas, respectively.

Only 18.7% of the labor force is wage earners, with 32.2% of men and only 5.6% of women being engaged in wage employment activities. The percent of wage employment is, however, higher in urban areas, with 39.6% of men and 10% of women in wage employment. Unemployment rate is high, with 18.7% of the labor force being unemployed. The unemployment rate is high among women, with approximately one third of women (32.7%) being unemployed compared to 13.6% of men. Higher rates of unemployment are noted in rural areas, perhaps reflecting the dependency on an intermittent and seasonal nature of employment, and the low employment opportunities in these areas.

The educational attainment is about 4 years for both men and women. Educational attainment is higher in urban areas than rural areas and higher among men than women. Thus men in urban areas have average years of education of about 7 and women 5.8 years. In rural areas average years of school attainment is only 3.7 for men and 2.4 for women. Educational attainment among wage earners is higher with an average of 5.6 years for both men and women. But women wage earners have higher average years of education, about 8 years, compared to 5 years for men.

The proportion of individuals in the labor force age 15-64 who obtained any form of vocational education or training is very low, at 3%. The proportion among men is higher, about 4% compared to 2.3% among women. The proportion with vocational education among wage earners is higher at 5%. More women wage earners have vocational training with the proportion among them at 7.7% compared to 5% among men wage earners. Urban areas have more persons with vocational qualifications compared to rural areas with 9.6% of women and 6.6% of men.

Among the wage employees men tend to be more experienced than women with an average year of experience of 22 years for men and women.

Table 1: Characteristics of Population Ages 15-64 and Of the Wage Earners Sample by Location and Sex

	Urban		Rural		All		Both sex
	Men	Women	Men	Women	Men	Women	
All persons age16-64:	4382	4400	8300	8881	12682	13281	25963
Years of education	6.909	5.758	3.663	2.411	4.784	3.520	4.138
Proportions with:							
Potential experience	19.353	19.510	21.529	21.460	20.777	20.814	20.796
Rural Resident	0.000	0.000	1.000	1.000	0.654	0.669	0.662
Vocational education	0.052	0.038	0.032	0.015	0.039	0.023	0.031
Proportion in labor force	0.745	0.231	0.805	0.288	0.784	0.269	0.521
Unemployment rate	0.118	0.303	0.145	0.336	0.136	0.327	0.187
Proportion of wage earners	0.396	0.100	0.283	0.035	0.322	0.056	0.186
Wage earners sample:	1737	439	2347	310	4084	749	4833
Years of	7.040	9.210	3.750	6.160	5.150	7.960	5.585

education							
Potential experience	21.85	19.46	23.12	20.99	22.58	20.09	22.20
Rural resident					0.575	0.414	0.550
Vocational education	0.066	0.096	0.041	0.052	0.051	0.077	0.055
Log monthly wage rate	5.732	5.587	5.311	5.057	5.490	5.367	5.471
Monthly wage	408.419	344.431	274.873	238.690	331.673	300.666	326.868

The distribution of the sample by education level, age and gender is shown in table 2. There are wide variation in educational attainment between men and women, favoring men. The proportion of uneducated males is much lower, 40.4 % compared to 57.6% of females. A higher percent of men has secondary and higher education, 20% and 6%, respectively, compared to 15% and 4.8% of females. The percent of men with primary education (at all level) is higher, at about 18% compared to 13% women. There are also wide difference in education attainment for the young and old age cohorts for men and women for all levels of education with clear improvement in favor of the young age cohort less than 35 years of age. For the latter, men and women have almost the same proportion with higher education; 6.2% and 5.9%. For women in particular, the proportion attaining higher level of education for the young age cohort (less than 35 years) is much higher compared with the old age cohort (5.9 percent compared to less than 2 percent). This improvement points to the increasing educational opportunities for females at higher education. For men the proportion with higher education remained the same for the different age cohorts at about 6%. Regarding primary attainment, though the proportion of the young age cohorts (less than 35 years) is much higher for men, 21% compared to women of about 16%, the latter has shown a conspicuous improvement from the lower proportion of 7.5% for the old age cohort 45-64.

Table 2: Distribution by Education, Age and Gender (%)

Men	age 15-34	age35-44	age 45-64	All
no education	34.03	46.36	52.32	40.41
Khalwa	3.47	6.23	10.66	5.59
incomplete primary	7.51	3.37	0.92	5.27
primary4	3.97	2.65	8.93	4.83
primary6	10.13	8.88	3.68	8.46
primary8	7.00	1.01	0.32	4.39
junior secondary	2.18	9.89	7.19	4.74
some/complete secondary	25.54	15.58	9.57	20.12
Post- secondary	6.17	6.02	6.41	6.20
Total	100	100	100	100
Total Observation	7484	2375	2823	12682
Women				
no education	48.38	67.04	79.79	57.62
Khalwa	2.05	2.25	2.88	2.24
incomplete primary	5.97	1.74	0.85	4.24
primary4	2.59	1.86	4.79	2.84
primary6	6.93	5.51	2.29	5.83
primary8	6.40	0.89	0.42	4.27

junior secondary	1.76	6.48	3.13	2.92
some/complete secondary	20.05	10.20	3.90	15.26
post-secondary	5.88	4.03	1.78	4.80
Total	100	100	100	100
Total Observations	8341	2579	2361	13281

Table 3 presents the distribution for the sub-sample of wage earners [3]. In contrast to table 1the differences in educational attainment between men and women favors the latter. Women wage employment participation increases with educational attainment. There are few women wage employees with no education compared to men. Only 33.5% of women wage earners are illiterate compared to almost 42% of men. The proportion of women employees with secondary and high (post-secondary) education is higher, 25% and 27%, compared with men percent of 18 and 9.8, respectively. In particular the young age cohort of women wage employees has higher percent with high education compared to men of the same age group. Women with post-secondary education constituted 32% of the total compared to only 8.4% of men with this level of education. On average wage-earning women has about 8 years of education, which is higher than an average of 5 years for male wage earners.

Table 3: Distribution by Education, Age and Gender for the Subsample of Wage Earners

Men	age 15-34	age35-44	age 45-64	All
no education	41.17	40.83	43.65	41.74
Khalwa	4.19	2.84	7.38	4.70
incomplete primary	8.68	3.95	1.12	5.56

primary4	1.33	2.74	8.22	3.48
primary6	5.37	8.00	4.67	5.83
primary8	7.40	1.12	0.37	4.04
junior secondary	3.60	10.33	9.25	6.71
some/complete secondary	19.82	19.66	13.55	18.14
post-secondary	8.43	10.54	11.78	9.82
Total	100	100	100	100
Total Observation	2028	987	1070	4085
Women				
no education	30.03	30.13	47.62	33.51
Khalwa	1.10	0.42	0.68	0.80
incomplete primary	5.23	1.67		3.07
primary4	0.55	0.42	5.44	1.47
primary6	4.68	2.93	1.36	3.47
primary8	2.48	1.67		1.74
junior secondary	1.93	5.44	5.44	3.74
some/complete secondary	21.76	32.64	21.09	25.10
post-secondary	32.23	24.67	18.37	27.10
Total	100	100	100	100
Total Observations	363	239	147	749

The Distribution of Earnings:

Means, standard deviations and median monthly earnings in SDG are shown separately for men in table 4a and women in table 4b for different education levels and age groups. Earnings include both cash and in-kind payments. No data is collected on other wage payments that top up the monthly wages like allowances and perks that have become wide spread among civil services and public employees in the recent years. A similarly important element that contribute to wage inequalities and which the data do not measure is earnings from the secondary jobs which is also an observed phenomenon in the labor market in Sudan. Nom account in the wage measure is also taken of social security payments.

Generally, earnings increase with the level of education at all age groups and with age at all educational levels. Men with post- secondary level of education earn 62% more compared with those with only secondary education. Depending on the type of primary education attended, men wages with this level of education are 28%-34% higher than wages earned by those with incomplete primary or no education.

Women monthly earnings are also lower at all educational levels compared with men's earnings. Overall, the wage differential by gender is not considerable. Mean monthly earnings for women is SDG 326.8 compared with SDG 331.6 for men. Differences are, however, larger at higher post- secondary education, with women earning on average SDG 415.7 monthly compared with monthly earnings of SDG 633.1 for men. Wage earnings of women with post- secondary education are thus 66 percent of their males' counterpart. Among women those with post -secondary degree have wages which are only 14% higher than those with secondary level of education. The wage differential among women is, however, higher between women with primary level of education and women with incomplete primary or no education. The gap is in the range of 39%-64% between the two groups.

Table 4a:Monthly Earning by Education, Age and Gender for the Subsample of Wage Earners in SDG:

Men	age 15-34	age35-44	age 45-64	All Ages
no education	233.71 (203.46) [200]	276.25 (227.38) [240]	271.41 (216.83) [220]	254.09 (213.83) [200]
Khalwa	287.76 (231.73) [240]	280.11 (147.94) [250]	291.82 (217.41) [280]	288.32 (214.54) [250]
incomplete primary	241.56 (162.13) [240]	277.28 (165.65) [260]	382.58 (241.68) [360]	255.154 (170.01) [240]
primary4	225.63 (177.88) [150]	407.04 (279.66) [300]	354.22 (206.31) [300]	339.81 (223.63) [300]
primary6	262.54 (180.86) [210]	354.54 (251.91) [290]	420.6 (318.55) [360]	326.29 (246.54) [252.5]
primary8	272.31 (181.76) [245]	352 (147.15) [360]	420 (266.33) [340]	281.2 (183.06) [250]
junior secondary	270.86 (136.64) [250]	339.07 (215.55) [300]	385.77 (202.94) [360]	337.77 (197.31) [300]

some/complete secondary	325.74	407.47	546.95	390.42
	(204.96)	(260.55)	(442.74)	(292.86)
	[300]	[358]	[480]	[332]
post-secondary	478.32	605.09	866.42	633.15
	(396.95)	(522.82)	(731.69)	(576.41)
	[380]	[455]	[700]	[500]
All Levels	281.16	354.02	406.49	331.59
	(230.440	(294.69)	(403.08)	(304.46)
	[240]	[300]	[300]	[280]

Note: Means are shown in the first entry for each level of education, standard deviation in parentheses and median in brackets.

Table 4b: Monthly Earning by Education, Age and Gender for the Subsample of Wage Earners in SDG:

Women	age 15-34	age35-44	age 45-64	All
no education	166.63 (280.05) [112]	196.25 (135.58) [160]	178.26 (113.62) [179.5]	178.37 (206.92) [150]
Khalwa	122.5 (74.11) [140]	25 . [25]	825 . [825]	223.33 (302.81) {140]
incomplete primary	184.16 (112.91) [150]	167.75 (79.122) [50]	.	181.30 (106.420 [150]
primary4	550 (353.55) [550]	50 . [50]	257.75 (173.72) [216]	292 (231.80) [232]
primary6	227 (167.71) [180]	303.29 (183.82) [264]	235 (21.214) [235]	248.15 (165.22) [210]
primary8	195.56 (118.23) [160]	399 (402.75) [223]	.	258.15 (243.76) [196]
junior secondary	316.57 (274.94) [232]	327.77 (125.01) [324]	336.88 (89.64) [325]	327.57 (160.880 [312]

some/complete secondary	297.48	379.45	491.81	363.53
	(236.25)	(178.800	(230.36)	(222.79)
	[280]	[380]	[500]	[300]
post-secondary	375.70	406.86	608.15	415.67
	(312.13)	(134.54)	(228.25)	(271.570
	[340]	[25]	[600]	[380]
All Levels	279.69	347.37	398.63	326.80
	(238.71)	(276.47)	(388.08)	(296.56)
	[248]	[300]	[300]	[280]

The distribution of wage earnings in urban and rural areas and for males and female are presented in table 5. Two summary measures of wage income inequality are also computed, the Gini coefficient and the logarithmic variance. Overall, the highest wage earners share in total wage income is more than 8 times the share of the lowest wage earnings individuals. A Gini concentration ration of 0 .37 is computed for overall wage distribution. The highest wage inequality is observed in rural areas compared with wage inequality in urban areas. On the other hand, males wage inequality is higher than females.

Table 5: Distribution of Wage Income, Sudan 2009

Urban		Rural		Males		Females		All	
% individuals	% of income	% individuals	% of income	% individuals	% of income	% individuals	% of income	% individuals	% of income
12.68	2.52	27.93	8.06	20.49	4.94	24.17	5.65	21.06	5.04
13.92	6.52	23.30	15.55	19.61	10.74	16.15	9.96	19.08	10.63
23.07	16.13	20.51	20.79	21.84	18.15	20.69	18.88	21.66	18.25
23.62	22.92	15.69	22.23	18.36	21.26	24.17	30.69	19.26	22.61
26.70	51.92	12.57	33.36	19.69	44.91	14.82	34.83	18.93	43.47
100	100	100.00	100.00	100.00	100.00	100.00	100.00	100.00	100
Gini coefficient (%)	33.4	38.0		39.5		31.1		37.2	
Variance of log wage	0.663	0.754		0.726		0.912		0.756	
Mean	395.50	270.65		331.67		300.66		326.87	
Sample	2176	2657		4084		749		4833	

It is noted from table5 that the lowest 25.6% wage earners in urban areas appropriates around 9% of total urban income whereas in rural areas the share of the lowest 27.9% in total rural income is only about 8%. On the other hand the top 26.7% of urban wage earners has an income share reaching 51.9% whereas in rural areas 28.3% at the top get 55.6% of total rural income. Gini coefficients are 38% and 33.4% for rural areas and urban areas, respectively. Perhaps this moderate or low level of inequality can be due in some part to the imprecision of measured wage variable, due to omission of non- reported part of income earnings as we cautioned before.

4. Estimates of Education Returns:

In this section the estimation results of the wage function are presented. Two specification of the basic wage function are presented in table 6 and table 7. In these specification years of education together with experience and its quadratic are entered as explanatory factors for change in wages. The wage differential between rural and urban areas is introduced through a dummy for residents in rural areas. In table 5 in addition, dummies for the state of residence are introduced, to distinguish between residence in one of the states in the Northern, Eastern, Central, Kordofan and Darfur regions against residence in Khartoum. Additional dummies are also included to test for the effect of vocational training and differential for the different age cohorts.

In both specifications, the effect of years of schooling is positive and statistically significant. The proportionate increase in wages associated with an additional year of schooling is higher for females than males. Also, for both sexes, the increase in wages associated with schooling is higher in rural areas compared to urban areas. In table 5 returns to an additional year of schooling are 7.7% and 5.1% for females and males, respectively. In rural areas the returns are highest to females, 10.5% compared to returns to males of 5.7%. In rural areas the returns are lower but women still realize a high wage premium of 5.5% compared to 4.5% for males. Wages in rural areas are also lower than in urban areas as evidenced by the negative coefficient in the dummy for residence in rural areas.

When region residence dummies are introduced (table 7) these rates of return are reduced. Wages are lower in all regions compared with Khartoum. The largest differential exists for states in Kordofan followed by those in Northern, Darfur, Eastern and Central regions, respectively. The reduction in returns is higher for females than males and it is observable more in urban areas. An additional year of education results in a proportionate increase in wages of 6.2% for females and 4.7% for males. In rural areas females realize a proportionate increase in wages for an additional schooling year of 8.9% whereas males realize only 5.3%. The returns to males in urban areas are now higher at 4%, than the returns to females of 3.6%.

The wage function is linear and quadratic in experience, with estimated coefficients that are significantly different from zero and with expected signs. In the specification with controls for regions an additional year of experience raises wages by 2.4% for females and 3% for males. Experience has a larger impact on wage variation for males residing in urban areas, whereas females get a higher premium on experience in rural areas. As with education some of the impact of experience in wages may be reflecting additional benefits associated with wage differential in different regions as the returns to experience are lower with regional controls. Vocational training tends to have a beneficial effect on wages, with individuals receiving any vocational training or qualification having additional wage increases as indicated by the positive coefficient on the dummy for vocational training. Old age cohorts (over 44 years) enjoy higher wage earnings compared with individuals who are less than 35 years old. On the other hand, those in middle age (35-44) have no advantage over the young age groups regarding wages.

The effect of education on wage differentials is examined further by introducing the different levels of education attained by the individuals. The effect of education on wages is approximated by the education spline shown in equation 5 which distinguishes between six levels of education, three for primary level and two for secondary levels (junior and senior) and post-secondary (for diplomas and university). Primary level takes 4, 6 or 8 years, junior secondary 3-4 years and secondary 3-4 years and diplomas and university 3 and 4 years, respectively. In other words, individual with 4 years of higher education who attended primary level with 4 grades (primary4), are assigned a value of 4 for their higher education variable, 4 years for junior secondary (intermediate level) and 4 years for senior (high) secondary.

The ordinary least square estimates of the spline (equation 7) are shown in table 8. The positive influence of education on wage changes is confirmed with these estimates and the returns to different education levels are recouped in table 8. Men obtain a return for additional year of primary education ranging from 3.5%-4.9% and a higher return of 5.6% on post-secondary level. Women education returns are higher than men, with proportionate increase in wages of 4.8%-8.5% for each year of primary education and lower returns of 6% on post- secondary education. Among primary education returns are higher for primary level with 4 years of education (primary4) followed by those who completed 6 years primary and then those with 8 years of completed primary schooling. This pattern is also observed for women.

Returns are generally higher in rural areas compared to urban areas at all levels of education. For women, in particular, the differential returns between rural and urban areas are high compared to men. Among women, in rural areas returns are 10%, 13.7% and 5.6% for 4years, 6years and 8years' primary level of education compared to 6.3%, 1.3% and 3.4% in urban areas. Women with post -secondary degrees earn 8.6% and 3.5% for each year in rural an urban areas, respectively. Men, on the other hand earn 5%, 4.1% and 5.2% for each year of primary4, primary6, and primay8 in rural areas compared, respectively, to 4.3%, 3.3 and 1.9% in urban areas.

As in the basic model experience enters with linear and quadratic term and the estimated coefficients are statically significant, with the exception of the estimated coefficients for women residing in urban areas. The coefficients on experience indicate that males' earnings peak at 36.5 years of experience or at age 48 whereas women peak earnings occur after 26.5 years of experience or at age 40 [4]. In rural areas women earnings peak after 38 years of experience or at age 46.

In rural areas wages are lower, as indicated by the estimates in the first two columns in table 8. For males wages are 21% lower in rural areas than urban areas, and for women wages are 26% lower [5]. Regarding the impact of vocational training, men and women receive above average wages compared with other workers with no vocational qualifications. Men and women with some vocational training receive, respectively, 15% and 23% increase in average wages compared with those with no training and the difference is statistically significant. However, the difference in average wages due to vocational training is not statistically significant in rural areas and for women in urban areas. This may be attributed to the type of vocational qualifications obtained that might be suited more for some jobs in services sector of urban areas than in rural areas.

Regional controls for residence shown in table 8 indicated the differences in wages in residing in state in any of the five areas compared to residence in Khartoum. The estimated coefficients are negative, and highly significant for all areas except for women in rural areas, but the estimated coefficients are found to be jointly significant at 4 percent level of significance. They show that for males in urban areas average wages are 34%, 26%, 21%, 20% and 16% lower, respectively, in states in the Northern, Kordofan, Eastern, Central and Darfur regions compared with urban areas of Khartoum. For men in rural areas the difference is highest in average wages in Kordofan and Darfur being 41% and 40% lower than rural Khartoum, respectively; and followed by the Northern region, 35%, central region, 33% and Eastern region 26%. For females in urban areas wages are 36%, 30%, 25% lower than in Khartoum in Central , Northern and Eastern states and the difference is statistically significant; however, for females resident in Kordofan and Darfur urban areas a difference of 18% and 9% is noticed but is not statistically significant.

Table 6: Ordinary Least Square Estimates of the wage Function (Dependent Variable Log Monthly Wage Rate)

	All		Urban		Rural	
	Males	Females	Males	Females	Males	Females
Constant	4.92	4.35	4.85	4.71	4.73	3.57
	(98.7)	(33.9)	(70.3)	(31.2)	(74.9)	(17.6)
Years of Schooling	0.051	0.077	0.045	0.055	0.057	0.105
	(22.0)	(14.2)	(13.8)	(7.95)	(17.4)	(12.4)
Experience	0.032	0.042	0.043	0.028	0.024	0.067
	(8.75)	(4.73)	(7.83)	(2.69)	(4.76)	(4.38)
Experience$^2 \times 10^{-2}$	-0.041	-0.057	-0.059	-0.037	-0.028	-0.097
	(-5.97)	(-3.32)	(-5.61)	(-1.76)	(-3.00)	(-3.41)
Rural	-0.272	-0.319	--	--	--	--
	(-10.5)	(-5.17)				
AdjustedR^2	0.169	0.281	0.123	0.133	0.118	0.343
F(K,N-K)	209.1	74.08	82.27	23.34	105.3	54.69
Sample	4084	749	1737	439	2347	310

Note: Absolute value of t-ratios in parentheses.

Table 7: Ordinary Least Square Estimates of the wage Function

(Dependent Variable Log Monthly Wage Rate)

	All		Urban		Rural	
	Males	Females	Males	Females	Males	Females
Constant	5.20	4.83	5.12	5.37	5.19	3.57
	(77.3)	(26.7)	(55.5)	(25.9)	(44.3)	(8.86)
Years of Schooling	0.047	0.062	0.040	0.036	0.053	0.089
	(17.1)	(8.47)	(10.9)	(4.02)	(13.9)	(7.37)
Experience	0.030	0.024	0.039	-0.002	0.023	0.065
	(6.76)	(2.03)	(5.71)	(-0.121)	(3.95)	(3.19)
Experience$^2 \times 10^{-2}$	-0.043	-0.050	-0.059	-0.022	-0.031	-0.099
	(-5.68)	(-2.61)	(-5.23)	(-0.964)	(-2.98)	(-3.04)
Vocational	0.142	0.202	0.176	0.148	0.095	0.149
	(2.53)	(1.79)	(2.38)	(1.18)	(1.13)	(0.681)
Age35-44	0.031	0.210	0.040	0.389	0.024	-0.048
	(0.75)	(1.97)	(0.621)	(3.07)	(0.426)	(-0.269)
Age45-64	0.103	0.403	0.125	0.594	0.075	0.096
	(1.59)	(2.39)	(1.30)	(2.97)	(0.845)	(0.338)
Rural	-0.226	-0.294	-			
	(-8.35)	(-4.52)				
Northern	-0.315	-0.065	-0.434	-0.358	-0.421	0.416
	(-6.23)	(-.567)	(-6.39)	(-2.77)	(-4.28)	(1.29)
Eastern	-0.269	-0.285	-0.228	-0.296	-0.446	0.035
	(-5.64)	(-2.53)	(-4.21)	(-2.61)	(-4.40)	(0.103)

Central	-0.253	-0.292	-0.218	-0.450	-0.421	0.218
	(-5.64)	(-2.84)	(-3.84)	(-2.61)	(-4.41)	(0.692)
Kordofan	-0.368	-0.349	-0.296	-0.179	-0.535	-0.129
	(-6.51)	(-2.86)	(-3.88)	(-1.30)	(-5.12)	(-0.392)
Darfur	-0.302	-0.199	-0.170	-0.075	-0.532	0.0269
	(-5.70)	(-1.76)	(-2.53)	(-0.599)	(-5.19)	(0.084)
AdjustedR^2	0.180	0.296	0.145	0.186	0.127	0.351
F(K,N-K)	75.73	27.17	27.73	10.08	31.99	16.22
Sample	4084	749	1737	439	2347	310

Note: Absolute value of t-ratios in parentheses.

Table 8: Ordinary Least Square Estimates of the wage Function

(Dependent Variable Log Monthly Wage Rate)

	Both Sex		Urban		Rural	
	Men	Women	Men	Women	Men	Women
Constant	5.15	4.82	5.03	5.36	5.15	3.62
	(75.4)	(25.7)	(53.3)	(24.7)	(43.5)	(8.34)
Primary4	0.049	0.085	0.043	0.063	0.050	0.100
	(2.85)	(1.35)	(1.63)	(0.86)	(2.25)	(0.84)
Primary6	0.039	0.062	0.033	0.013	0.041	0.137
	(4.38)	(2.18)	(2.42)	(0.39)	(3.44)	(2.59)
Primary8	0.035	0.048	0.019	0.034	0.052	0.056
	(4.26)	(1.62)	(1.67)	(0.96)	(4.39)	(1.09)
Junior Secondary	0.030	0.070	0.023	0.034	0.034	0.120
	(5.14)	(3.69)	(2.86)	(1.60)	(3.95)	(3.14)
Secondary	0.046	0.067	0.037	0.041	0.054	0.092
	(12.9)	(7.58)	(7.66)	(3.85)	(10.5)	(5.85)
Post-Secondary	0.056	0.060	0.053	0.035	0.060	0.086
	(17.5)	(7.82)	(12.3)	(3.69)	(11.7)	(6.50)
Vocational	0.139	0.210	0.156	0.163	0.106	0.139
	(2.49)	(1.85)	(2.13)	(1.29)	(1.26)	(0.61)
Experience	0.038	0.026	0.051	0.0007	0.029	0.061
	(8.24)	(2.05)	(7.22)	(0.05)	(4.81)	(2.82)
$Experience^2 \times 10^{-2}$	-0.051	-0.049	-0.070	-0.023	-0.038	-0.089

	(-6.61)	(-2.45)	(-6.09)	(-0.95)	(-3.65)	(-.60)
Age35-44	-0.034	0.176	-0.066	0.355	-0.016	-0.021
	(-0.80)	(1.60)	(-1.00)	(2.69)	(-0.29)	(0.11)
Age45-64	-0.004	0.317	-0.064	0.524	0.024	0.035
	(-0.07)	(1.79)	(-0.65)	(2.47)	(0.27)	(0.12)
Rural	-0.236	-0.298				
	(-8.75)	(-4.57)				
Northern	-0.315	-0.066	-0.420	-0.359	-0.425	0.422
	(-6.25)	(-0.57)	(-6.27)	(-2.76)	(-4.32)	(1.21)
Eastern	-0.276	-0.274	-0.239	-0.286	-0.443	-0.035
	(-5.82)	(-2.41)	(-4.49)	(-2.50)	(-4.36)	(-0.09)
Central	-0.246	-0.295	-0.217	-0.452	-0.405	0.212
	(-5.34)	(-2.84)	(-3.88)	(-4.18)	(-4.23)	(0.62)
Kordofan	-0.368	-0.375	-0.296	-0.194	-0.529	-0.179
	(-6.55)	(-3.06)	(-3.92)	(-1.40)	(-5.05)	(-.51)
Darfur	-0.290	-0.192	-0.175	-0.092	-0.506	0.055
	(-5.50)	(-1.69)	(-2.64)	(-0.72)	(-4.92)	(0.16)
Adjusted R^2	.18	.29	0.169	0.179	0.126	0.340
F(K,N-K)	56.84	19.10	23.16	7.00	22.16	10.97
Sample	4084	749	1737	439	2347	310

Note: Absolute value of t-ratios in parentheses.

Table 9: Proportionate Returns to Different Levels of Education by Gender and Location (%)

	Men			Women		
Education level	Urban	Rural	All	Urban	Rural	All
Primary4	4.3	5.0	4.9	6.3	10.0	8.5
Primary6	3.3	4.1	3.9	1.3	13.7	6.2
Primary8	1.9	5.2	3.5	3.4	5.6	4.8
Junior Secondary	2.3	3.4	3.0	3.4	12.0	7.0
Some/complete Secondary	3.7	5.4	4.6	4.1	9.2	6.7
Post-Secondary	5.3	6.0	5.6	3.5	8.6	6.0

Note: These are compiled from the estimated regression in table 7.

Returns to different levels of education are shown for three age cohorts in table 10. The breakdown by age cohort reduces the number of observation for estimating returns, particularly for women, and might affect the precision of the estimates. Also, there might be some data errors in reported age that could lead to some individuals being misplaced in a particular age-education level. Thus those who reported completed primary level of the 4 years system and whose age is in the range 15-34 might actually be reporting incomplete primary level of education of 4 years or giving an incorrect younger age [6]. Nevertheless, the results are suggestive.

For men in the old cohort (45-64) the proportionate returns to an additional year of school at the primary level is 6.7%-8.4%. It is 4.5% at the middle, 6% at the high school levels and 7.7% at the post-secondary level. Thus, returns increase slightly with the level of education. Generally, however, the returns for the cohort 45-64 are higher than for younger age cohort 35-34 at all levels of education. For women in the cohort 45-64 the reverse is observed with returns higher at the primary level, 4.3%- 8.1% compared to 3.8 at the post- secondary level. Also, the returns to younger cohorts 15-34 are higher than for the old cohort 45-64 for all education levels.

Table 10: Proportionate Returns to Different Levels of Education by Gender and Cohort (%)

	Men			Women		
Education level	15-34	35-44	45-64	15-34	35-44	45-64
Primary4	-3.1	9.7	6.7	8.7	---	8.1
Primary6	1.9	4.0	8.4	6.1	6.2	4.3
Primary8	3.1	--	--	4.2	---	
Junior Secondary	2.4	3.0	4.5	6.7	5.9	4.8
Some/complete Secondary	4.3	4.2	6.0	7.2	5.3	4.3
Post- Secondary	4.8	5.3	7.7	5.8	4.3	3.8

Note: These are computed using the regression in table a3 in the appendix.

The declining rates of return for the youngest male cohort compared to the old aged cohort 45-64 implies that rates of return might have declined over time for males due to increased supply of educated males. For females, on the other hand, the higher rates of return for the youngest cohort could signify an increased demand for more educated females in the face of a constraint supply.

The estimated rates of return shown in table 6 and table 7 are low and inconsistent with the world pattern of levels reported by Psacharopouls (1994). The latter reported an average rate of return for an additional year of education of 10%, and an average rate of return for men of 20.1%, 13.9%, and 13.4% to primary, secondary and higher education. For women the average reported rates to primary, secondary and higher education are 12.8%, 18.4%, and 12.7%.

Cohen and House (1994) study found also similar low returns for primary education of 4.6% in Khartoum but higher returns to university level of 12.6%. However, Kunaa (2003) used the Migration and Labor Force Survey 1996, and arrived at much higher rates of returns using the Mincerian function, and higher rates for university compared to primary level. For the primary level, a rate of 14% is estimated compared with a higher rate for the university level of 18%. Returns were also higher for women compared to men; with university level rates standing at 22% for women compared to 16% for women. As for primary level women obtained a premium of 33% compared with 10% for men.

Assad (1997) finds also low returns to primary education in Egypt, ranging from 2.3%-3.7% for females to 4.0%-8.0% to men and 8.2%-8.8% for higher education, depending on whether the individual is employed in the private or public sector. Similarly, low returns have been found in Morocco (Lane, hakim and Miranda, 1999) and Kuwait (Chishti and Khalaf, 2000).

It is hypothesized that the low returns can be explained by compression of pay scales in the non- competitive public sector which flattens mean earnings differentials and hence depresses return (Psacharopouls, 1994). In the Sudan a compression of wages in the civil service has been occurring but the data used in this analysis does not allow a break by sector of employment to make possible separate estimates for the public and the private sector[7].

The reduction of wage rents in the non- competitive public sector may not be the sole explanation for the reduced returns to education since it is equally likely that the forces of competition in the private sector has acted in such a manner as to reduce wages. It is noted that in the last two decades the employment opportunities in the public sector has become scarce due to budgetary restraints and curtailment of employment and privatization, with an increasing reliance on the private sector for creation of employment. Limited by size, low investment and low productivity the formal sector was unable to absorb an increasing supply of educated labor market entrants resulting from the tremendous expansion in education in the beginning of the 90s and onward, particularly at the higher level, leading to the observed high levels of unemployment, especially among college graduates. It is estimated that during the inter-census period 1993-2008 employment has been growing at less than one per cent per annum, (0.9%) and at a rate lower than a growth rate of the labor force of 1.3% (CBS, 2008). With an excess supply of graduates, competition in the private sector would bid down wages resulting in low returns.

Secondly, the structural transformation of the economy that accompanied the inception of oil production in the Sudan in 1999 led to expansion of non-tradable sectors in transport, construction and home services and domestic trade activities, with consequently increasing demand for unskilled and "blue" collar wage occupations and increased demand for informal urban private sector occupations, raising pay of those engaging in these sectors. At the same time, paucity of job opportunities in the formal and government sectors which are the main employers of "white" collar work probably have led to stagnant real wages for this group and, therefore, the narrowing of wage differences between those with low and high levels of education and the observed low inequality in wage earnings and the low proportionate returns from education noted in this analysis[8].

5. Estimates Corrected for Selectivity Bias:

Table 11 and table 12 presents the estimates corrected for selectivity bias using Heckman two stage least squares for males and females, respectively. The tables show the estimates of the probit for wage earners and the logarithmic wage function. As identifying variables for the probit function I have used land ownership by the household (whether fully owned or partially owned), and access to communal land; and these enter as dummy variables. They also included non-earned household income per adult equivalent, which is composed of income from property, transfers from non-resident household members inside and outside Sudan, and social governmental and non- governmental support [9].

In column 3 the estimated marginal effects of the probit for males, calculated at the means of the variables, are shown. The estimates show that the probability of choosing wage employment by males increases with the level of education and is positively and significantly associated with education level for those attaining primary8 (basic education) and above. The likelihood of wage employment is lower for those who attained primary 4 or primary6 level of education. As indicated by the estimates, one year of post-secondary education increases the probability of wage employment by about 2% while lower levels of education increases it by about 1%. Vocational education has a highly positive and statistically significant effect in participating in wage employment and it raises the probability of participation by about 6%.

Experience influences the choice of wage employment significantly and appears with linear and quadratic term, and the estimates imply that one year of potential experience increases the probability of wage employment by 0.8% and the probability reaches its peak at age 32. Also, individuals aged 35 years and over are less likely to participate in wage employment by 3%, as shown by the estimates of the age cohort dummies.

The likelihood of wage employment decreases significantly for those residing in rural areas where rural residence lowers probability of wage employment by 4.5%. Also, the probability of wage employment is lower in the western and eastern states compared to Khartoum, higher in the central states and not significantly different in the northern ones. As shown in the table residence in Darfur and Kordofan reduces the probability of wage employment choice by 10% and 3%, respectively.

The influence of the variables omitted from the wage earnings equation and used as identifiers of the probability function is shown to be highly significant, and these variables are negatively affecting the probability of an individual choosing wage employment. The highest impact is seen for land ownership whether fully, partially or communally owned. Owned land has the largest effect where a reduction of probability of wage employment of 11% - 13% is noted for individuals whom families own land. Communal land lowers the probability of wage occupation also, but by lower percentage compared to owned land (5.5%). Similarly, the probability of

Table 11: Estimates of Probit for Wage earners and the Logarithmic Earnings Equation for Men

Variable	Probit Wage Earner		Logarithmic Monthly Earnings
	Coefficient(t-ratio)	Marginal effect(t-ratio)	Coefficient(t-ratio)
Constant	-1.184(-17.7)	-.423 (-18.0)	5.784 (28.2)
Primary4	-.036 (-2.31)	-.013 (-2.31)	.056 (3.20)
Primary6	-.016 (-1.88)	-.005 (-1.88)	.043 (4.67)

Primary8	.043 (5.35)	.015 (5.35)	.022 (2.43)
Junior Secondary	.026 (3.99)	.009 (3.99)	.023 (3.53)
Secondary	.033 (8.93)	.012 (8.93)	.036 (8.05)
Post-Secondary	.047 (13.1)	.017 (13.05)	.044 (8.95)
Experience	.083 (19.4)	.029 (19.45)	.015 (1.81)
Experience$^2 \times 10^{-2}$	-.129 (-17.7)	-.046 (-17.8)	-.016 (-1.24)
Vocational	.156 (2.59)	.058 (2.52)	.102 (1.74)
Age35-44	-.091 (-2.00)	-.032 (-2.03)	-.009 (-.19)
Age45-64	-.080 (-1.13)	-.028 (-1.15)	.030 (.435)
Rural	-.125 (-4.33)	-.045 (-4.31)	-.174 (-5.23)
Northern	.027 (.506)	.009 (.504)	-.320 (-6.15)
Eastern	-.099 (-1.94)	-.035 (-1.97)	-.242 (-4.84)
Central	.164 (3.25)	.059 (3.21)	-.275 (-5.71)
Kordofan	-.083 (-1.42)	-.029 (-1.44)	-.304 (-4.98)
Darfur	-.293 (-5.37)	-.099 (-5.69)	-.182 (-2.84)
Non-earned income per adult equivalent$\times 10^{-2}$	-.006 (-2.62)	-.002 (-2.62)	
Owned land	-.370 (-12.2)	-.128 (-12.7)	
Partially owned land	-.355 (-3.82)	-.115 (-4.31)	
Communal land	-.160 (-3.71)	-.055 (-3.85)	
λ			-.380 (-3.25)
-log likelihood	7395.54		4689.9
X^2	1398.37		901.90
Adjusted R^2			0.190

Sample size	12682		4084

Participation in wage earning activities declines as per adult equivalent non-earned household income increases, but its impact is the lowest. One standard deviation increase in per adult non-earned income decreases the probability of wage employment by 1%. As argued before these variables raise the shadow wage of undertaking home or self-employment activities and therefore reduces the likelihood of being engaged in wage employment.

The OLS estimates of the log wage earnings function for males corrected for sample selection bias are shown in column 3 of table 11. The selection term λ appears with a negative and statistically significant coefficient, and hence uncorrected OLS estimates suffer from sample selection bias. It also suggests that those who select into wage employment are above average quality[10] i.e. those with lower than average characteristics engage` on home or own-account self-employment. The correction results in an increase in the estimated rates of return of primary education to 5.6% and 4.3% for primary4 and primary6 levels of education compared with the previously estimated levels of 4.9% and 3.9%, respectively, and a reduction in returns for other levels of education by at least one percentage point. Accordingly, returns from post-secondary education are now 4.4% compared to the previously estimated 5.6%, and hence lower than returns from primary education. Generally, however, the pattern of lower rates of return for all education levels prevails. The same pattern as in the uncorrected OLS estimates of the impact of location is observed here, with somewhat lower value of the estimated coefficients for some of the variables.

Female wage earners probit and log wage earnings are shown in table 12. From these estimates the probability of participating in wage employment increases with years of schooling for all education levels, and this association is statistically significant for all education levels with the exception of those with primary4 level, where only few numbers of women could have attained the latter level of education, which pertains to the old education system. It is also noted that additional year of education of high levels of education produces a larger impact on the probability of wage employment compared with the effect of low education levels. Thus, an additional year of post-secondary or secondary education increases the probability of participating in wage employment by 1 percent compared to the impact of additional years of primary education of 0.8 percent.

Experience influences the female's wage employment probability significantly and enters with linear and quadratic terms, with one year of additional experience raising the probability by 0.3 percent. As for vocational education, a large percentage significant impact of 6.5% is noted on the females' probability of choosing wage employment for those who had some form of it.

Location tends to have a significant impact on engaging in wage labor by females. Female wage labor tend to be less likely in rural areas compared to urban areas, which should be expected since domestic and own account employment is the dominant form of occupations for females in rural areas. Thus, given other factors such as areas of residence and the related socio-economic environment, females in rural areas are about 3% less likely to engage in wage labor. As noted from the table, women in western and central regions are 1%-2% more likely to undertake wage employment compared to those residing in Khartoum, while the probability of undertaking wage jobs are lower in the northern and eastern regions but the difference is not statistically significant. Where agriculture is the dominant sector of employment as in the former regions, land is the main factor of production and it is ownership is critical in employment opportunities and income generation. This in fact is revealed by a significant and negative impact of land ownership on the probability of females engaging in wage labor. But, while the land ownership, and consequently secure land tenure, could possibly raise the shadow wage of own account work in agricultural areas for female, access to communally cultivated land produces an opposite positive impact on wage employment by females and hence encourages them to seek that alternative. Insecure land tenure (note also the positive impact of partially owned land and which might be not clearly defined in terms of tenure rights) and perhaps being unable to enjoy the full returns from working in a commonly owned land pool could be a cause of this outcome. Finally, non-earned household income does not seem to influence females' decisions to undertake wage labor.

Regarding the log wage earnings estimates for females which are corrected for sample selection, it is apparent from the last column of table 12 that the correction has not produced noticeable change regarding the estimated impact of education and most other variables using OLS. Primary education commands similar and highest returns of 5%-6% with a lower return for post-secondary education of 5%. As indicated by the effect of the correction term there appears to be no sample selection bias of females, since λ is not statistically significant. The effect of experience though, which was statistically significant in the OLS estimates, has a weak impact in the corrected estimate of the wage function, possibly being captured now by the probability term λ, where the probability of securing wage employment by females was found to be significantly related to experience. Therefore women with longer years of potential experience are more likely to be engaged in wage pay occupations relative to those engaged in other forms of employment.

Table 12: Estimates of Probit for Wage earners and the Logarithmic Earnings Equation for Females

	Probit Wage Earner		Logarithmic Monthly Wage
Variable	Coefficient(t-ratio)	Marginal effect(t-ratio)	Coefficient (t-ratio)
Constant	-2.81 (-24.5)	-.249 (-23.15)	5.07 (4.31)
Primary4	.002 (.059)	.0002 (.059)	.085 (1.36)
Primary6	.033 (2.11)	.003 (2.10)	.059 (1.95)
Primary8	.034 (2.21)	.003 (2.21)	.046 (1.49)
Junior Secondary	.026 (2.18)	.002 (2.18)	.068 (3.27)
Secondary	.091 (14.9)	.008 (14.8)	.061 (2.07)
Post-Secondary	.116 (21.2)	.010 (20.06)	.053 (1.47)
Experience	.086 (11.9)	.008 (12.2)	.020 (.70)
Experience$^2 \times 10^{-2}$	-.132 (-10.5)	-.012 (-10.5)	-.041 (-.92)
Vocational	.492 (5.51)	.065 (4.02)	.181 (1.03)
Age35-44	-.004 (-.056)	-.0003 (-.056)	.177 (1.63)

Age45-64	-.003 (-.024)	-.0002 (-.024)	.321 (1.83)
Rural	-.266 (-5.83)	-.026 (-5.40)	-.280 (92.5)
Northern	-.038 (-.48)	-.003 (-.49)	-.065 (-.57)
Eastern	-.046 (-.60)	-.004 (-.62)	-.272 (-2.41)
Central	.134 (1.83)	.012 (1.74)	-.305 (-2.72)
Kordofan	.141 (1.65)	.014 (1.52)	-.383 (-3.03)
Darfur	.212 (2.70)	.021 (2.42)	-.205 (-1.61)
Non-earned income per adult equivalent$\times 10^{-2}$	.0008 (.31)	.0007 (.31)	
Owned land	-.137 (-2.72)	-.012 (-2.81)	
Partially owned land	.045 (.33)	.004 (.32)	
Communal land	.198 (3.06)	.020 (2.70)	
λ			-.083 (-.21)
-log likelihood	2600.475		880.36
χ^2	1089.641		294.63
Adjusted R^2			.2905869
Sample size	13281		749

Decomposition of Male-Female Wage differences:

Table 13 presents the decomposition of total differential in mean wages between men and women for the sample and for the rural and urban sectors [11]. The overall average earnings advantage of men over women is 0.18 in log units or SDG 27.6. It is 0.14 in the urban areas, or SDG 41.7 and 0.25 in rural areas or SDG 45.0. The unexplained differential between male and female workers is large. Nearly 32% of earnings differential between males and females may be attributed to unexplained variation. This unexplained differential is caused primarily by a large difference in the intercept in favor of males, particularly in rural areas. This difference is largely mitigated by the superior human capital endowment and higher returns to females, with 24.7% of the differential being counteracted by the high returns to education of females and another 14.2% by their endowment of wage enhancing characteristics (longer years of education). A large impact of coefficients and wage endowment is noted in rural areas. In urban areas the positive returns working in favor of male worker characteristics are most probably due to the larger returns to potential years of experience of male workers compared to female workers; but these are counteracted by the superior female workers endowment of longer years of education.

Table 13: Decomposition of Male-Female Wage Differentials, Sudan 2009

		Component			
Log Wage Comparison	Total mean differential	(i) Worker endowment	(ii) Constant	(iii) Returns to worker characteristics	Total unexplained differential (ii) + (iii)
All sample	0.181	-0.142	0.570	-0.247	0.323
Urban	0.145	-0.066	0.134	0.077	0.211
Rural	0.252	-0.120	1.162	-0.790	0.372

Note; Calculations are based on the wage equations estimates of table 5. See equation 3 note 11 for decomposition formula.

6. Summary and Implications:

This chapter applied the standard human capital model in explaining wage earnings variation in Sudan, using the recent household budget survey (NBHS, 2009) data. The education and experience variables of the model were found to influence significantly the earnings differential of men and women in different locations.

Education was found to have a positive impact on wage differentials, and experience is related to earnings variation linear and quadratic form, as the model predicts. Women obtain a higher average return of around 8% for an additional year of education compared with 5% for men. This also holds for returns to different levels of education, where these are higher for women at all level of schooling compared to what men get from these level. For women proportionate returns are higher at the primary level compared to the higher levels of education. On the other hand returns to men are slightly higher at the secondary and post - secondary level.

These findings suggest a policy of expanding education opportunities for females at the primary level. Though females' primary enrollment has been expanding over the years the enrollment ratio of female to men has not reached equality. Moreover, since returns are higher at all levels of education in rural than urban areas, suggesting the scarcity of human capital in rural areas, and since the difference between rural and urban areas is larger for women than men, a policy that expands education opportunities for women at all levels of education, and particularly at the primary level is desirable on this basis. Also, the highest returns for women in the young age cohort, perhaps reflecting an increased demand for educated young women in the presence of scarce supply, lends support to this proposition. As indicated by the decomposition analysis of the female-male differential the higher returns and advantages in the human capital endowment of women works favorably to mitigate the wage differences between men and women that may be due to discrimination or biases in women employment and wage determination.

As for men, a reduction of returns to the young age cohorts is noted, compared with those in the old age cohort. An increasing supply of educated males resulting from the expansion of education opportunities, particularly at the high level of education, with scarce demand in the formal private sector and high unemployment rates for those with high education could be cause of these lower returns.

Another important suggestive result regards the impact of vocational training and qualification. Men and women with vocational training receive above average wages received by workers with the same years of education but without vocational training. The differential is higher for women compared to men; an increase of 23% in average wages of women compared to15% for men. However, vocational training seems to be effective in enhancing productivity in urban areas, and particularly of men. This is attributed to the kind of training programs offered and possibly the quality of these programs. Vocational training programs are oriented toward male occupations in mechanical, electrical, carpentry and bricklaying skills. This suggests a policy of expansion of vocational education and restructuring of the course contents to allow enrollment by more women.

Residential location is found to be an important factor in explaining wage differences. Wages for individuals located in rural areas were 20% lower than the average wages in urban areas. There are also wide variations in wages between residents of states in Khartoum and those in other region, with lower wages for those residing outside Khartoum. The difference is larger between rural residents in other regions and those residing in rural areas of Khartoum, ranging between 26%-40%. The difference between urban Khartoum and other urban areas ranges between 16% -34%. These results imply that rural-rural and rural-urban flows towards the country's centre will continue. Therefore, improving productivity and enhancing wages in the country side should be a priority of development efforts if a broad-based equitable and balanced growth is to be attained.

Correcting for sample selectivity bias, using Heckman two-stage least square, has not resulted in changing the low levels of returns obtained by OLS. However, for male wage earners an evidence of selectivity bias is noted, and the corrected estimates resulted in slightly upward adjustment of primary returns and a reduction on returns to post- secondary education. This may indicate that decisions regarding continuation to higher level of education and choice of joining labor market activities are inseparable for males as some individuals may decide to continue to higher levels of education in the face of rising unemployment. Future research in this area in Sudan should aim to understand the forces that may induce some individuals to 'park' at institutions of higher education as they wait an acceptable job offer.

Education was found to influence participation in wage employment positively and significantly for both men and women, with higher impact noted for the former. And vocational form of education tends to increase the likelihood of wage employment for both men and women, with stronger impact for the latter. This lends support to the importance of vocational training and enhancement and development of vocational education because of its beneficial impact of securing jobs.

Wage employment participation was affected negatively by alternative job opportunities resulting from land ownership and the non-earned household income. A high likelihood of engaging in wage labor by women from families that might enjoy access to communal land may be an indication of a need by some of those from conflict and draught stricken areas for alternative sources of livelihood as they lose access to these assets due to the calamities they face.

Finally, a remarkable characteristic of the rates of return revealed in this analysis is their low level and inconsistency with average patterns found in similar environments and with returns that were estimated for Sudan using data in the mid-nineties, particularly for those with high education. It is argued that declining recruitment of the educated by the public sector, in addition to compressed wage scales in the sector that led to low average wages, could be a reason for this outcome. Of equal importance is a surplus of unemployed graduates that could have led to depressed wages in the formal private sector and employment in lower-paid "blue" collar jobs by these graduates. An important institutional factor that contributed to low wages in formal sector activities is the dissolution of the professional and workers unions, which has historically stood behind demand for wage increases to preserve real wages and standard of living of employees, and their replacement by government- loyal associations and "enterprise" unions.

The set of data used in the analysis does not allow disaggregation by sector of employment and it is interesting to examine this issue using sets of data that allow this when it becomes available. Another thing which is also not undertaken in the analysis and which deserves treatment is the examination of the effect of the quality of education offered and their contribution to the observed low returns from education. Herein, it is interesting to note that returns to education from a 4-years primary system of education (primary4) are higher than the returns obtained from a 6-years primary education level (primary6). If wage differences represent differences in productivity then the 4-years primary system should be of better quality, and on this account the system of education on which primary schooling is composed of 4 years should be preferred. The latest decision by the Ministry of

Education to separate the primary8 level into two tiers, and to increase the secondary level years to 4 years instead of 3 years, is a step in the right direction.

Notes:

1. If forgone earnings represent only a fraction of education cost k_s which is not necessarily equal 1, the coefficient on schooling is given by $r = k_s r$, and the rate of return will be computed by dividing the estimated coefficient on s by k_s; for elaboration see Chiswick (1997).

2. Experience is measured as the lesser of:

X= Age– schooling years– school entry age

X= Age– 14

Where it is assumed that entry into labor market employment starts at age 14.

3. The employment status of female and male labor force ages 15-64 is as follows (%):

	male	female	Total
Paid employee	47.30	29.92	43.25
Employer	6.17	2.84	5.39
Own account worker	39.90	33.27	38.36
Unpaid family worker	6.52	33.75	12.86
Unpaid, working for others	0.11	0.22	0.14
Total	100	100	100
Total Number	8945	2714	11659

4. To calculate the years of experience for which lnw is greatest differentiate equation 4 with respect to X, sets the result equal to zero, and solve for X*. This yields the level of experience for which lnw is maximized

$X^* = -\beta_1/\beta_2$

5. In order to get the wage differential between rural and urban areas the estimated coefficient is exponentiated and is subtracted from 1 i.e. $1 - e^\beta$.

6. To achieve consistency between age and level of current school attended the CBS introduced a predefined acceptable age range with upper and lower cut-off for each level of school from primary 1 to University. People defined too old for a certain school level reported were considered as "not currently attending" and the initially reported school level was taken to mean the "highest ever school level" attended.

7. For instance the ratios of grade one pay (top civil servants), middle scale grade (grade 1V) and grade 1X (entry for university graduates) to the lowest grade pay (grade XV11) in the civil service declined, respectively, from 11, 7.6 and 2.4 in 1985 to 5.7, 4.5 and 2.3 in 1994.

8. The distribution of employees by sector of economic activity is as follows:

	Male	Female
	%	%
agriculture	17.62	11.64
manufacture, mining and quarrying	3.32	0.68
electricity and water	2.04	0.41
building and construction	11.53	1.35
trade, transport, restaurants, information and communication, finance, & other service	13.79	6.22
technical and professional	6.41	3.38
public administration, defense, education and health service	19.81	55.89
other	25.49	20.43
Total	100.00	100.00

As the table shows, over three quarters of female employees were employed in education, health service and public administration (56%) and other services, including home production and domestic services (20%). Half the male employees were in trade and restaurants, transport, finance and building and construction (25%) and other services including home production and services (25.5%). Only about a fifth of male employees were in public administration, health and education services and another 18% in agriculture.

9. It is assumed that the non-earned household income is not affected an any way by wage earnings of the individuals participants in wage labor, as for example via the transfers component, which is reasonable assumption given that these transfers are received from nonresidents household members. These transfers might be used in augmenting the household human capital and the individual education variables might be correlated with non-earned

income through the impact of transfers but this impact takes place over the long run, and therefore currently received transfers might not be reflecting this long run effect. The only impact of non-earned household income would be a wealth effect that raises the individual's reservation wage and reduces the participation in labor market.

10. The coefficient on the correction term λ is given by $\rho\sigma_u$, where ρ is the correlation coefficient between the error term of the wage function and the selection equation error term, and σ_u is the standard error of the wage function random error.

11. The methodology for decomposition may be outlined as follows (Oaxaca, 1973): Separate wage equations may be estimated for males and females as follows:

$$y^m = \alpha^m + \sum b_i^m X^m + \mu^m \quad (1)$$

$$y^f = \alpha^f + \sum b_i^f X^f + \mu^f \quad (2)$$

Where X represents a vector of the individuals characteristics, the b are their coefficients from the estimated wage equations; α is the constant term and the superscripts f and m indicate females and males workers, respectively. Evaluating equations (1) and (2) at the mean values for the characteristics, and then subtracting equation 2 from 1 and after some manipulation, we can write:

$$y^m - y^f = (\alpha^m - \alpha^f) + \sum b^m (\bar{X}^m - \bar{X}^f) + \sum \bar{X}^f (b^m - b^f) \quad (3).$$

Equation 3 decomposes the differential into three components (i) the difference in constant terms (ii) the difference in the observed worker characteristics; and (iii) the difference in the returns to worker characteristics. The first and the third components constitute the unexplained part of the mean wage differential. The second term represents the differential in endowment between the two groups.

Appendix

Table A1: Means and Standard Deviations of Variables in the sub-Sample of Wage Earners by Gender, 2009

	Males		Females	
	Mean	Standard deviation	Mean	Standard Deviation
Wage earner	1	0	1	0
Log wage	5.49	0.86	5.37	0.95
School Years	5.15	5.69	7.96	6.65
Primary4	0.14	0.73	0.06	0.48
Primary6	0.35	1.40	0.21	1.10
Primary8	0.32	1.57	0.14	1.04
Junior Secondary	0.60	2.23	0.33	1.69
Secondary	1.73	4.13	2.63	4.89
Post-Secondary	1.56	4.73	4.31	7.08
vocational	0.05	0.22	0.08	0.27
Experience	22.6	12.5	20.1	11.8
Experience^2 $\times 10^{-2}$	6.65	6.65	5.44	5.95
Age < 35	0.50	0.50	0.48	0.50
Age 35-44	0.24	0.43	0.32	0.47
Age 45-64	0.26	0.44	0.20	0.40
Primary4*Age35-44	0.03	0.32	0.005	0.15
Primary6*Age35-44	0.12	0.83	0.056	0.58
Primary8*Age35-44	0.02	0.41	0.043	0.58
Junior*Age35-44	0.22	1.40	0.155	1.17

Secondary*Age35-44	0.51	2.42	1.10	3.47
Post Sec*Age 35-44	0.40	2.51	1.25	4.28
Primary4*Age45-64	0.09	0.58	0.04	0.41
Primary6*Age45-64	0.07	0.66	0.016	0.31
Primary8*Age45-64	0.008	0.25	0	0
Junior*Age45-64	0.21	1.36	0.09	0.90
Secondary*Age45-64	0.39	2.13	0.48	2.35
Post Sec*Age45-64	0.49	2.74	0.57	2.94
Experience*Age35-44	5.94	10.9	7.31	11.4
Experience*Age45-64	10.1	17.4	7.14	15.0
Experience^2*Age35-44	1.54	3.06	1.82	3.23
Experience^2*Age45-64	4.05	7.52	2.76	6.38
Rural	0.57	0.49	0.41	0.49
Khartoum	0.10	0.30	0.13	0.34
Northern	0.16	0.37	0.15	0.36
Eastern	0.21	0.40	0.15	0.35
Central	0.31	0.46	0.26	0.44
Kordofan	0.10	0.29	0.12	0.33
Darfur	0.12	0.33	0.19	0.39
Married	0.66	0.47	0.73	0.44
Non Earned Household income	464.84	8859.28	659.40	4419.8
Owned land	0.24	0.43	0.22	0.41
Rent Land	0.08	0.28	0.09	0.28

Partially Owned Land	0.01	0.12	0.02	0.14
Communal Land	0.02	0.14	0.01	0.11
sample	4084		749	

Table A2: Means and Standard Deviations of Variables in the sub-Sample of Wage Earners by Gender, 2009

	Urban		Rural	
	Males	Female	Males	Females
Wage earner	1(0.0)	1(0.0)	1(0.0)	1(0)
Log wage	5.73(0.81)	5.59(0.82)	5.31(0.84)	5.05(1.04)
School Years	7.04(5.89)	9.21(6.30)	3.75(5.10)	6.19(6.75)
Primary4	0.13(0.71)	0.06(0.50)	0.14(0.75)	0.05(0.45)
Primary6	0.34(1.39)	0.25(1.19)	0.35(1.42)	0.15(0.95)
Primary8	0.40(1.75)	0.15(1.07)	0.26(1.42)	0.13(1.01)
Junior Secondary	0.74(2.46)	0.42(1.89)	0.49(2.03)	0.20(1.34)
Secondary	2.42(4.72)	3.05(5.16)	1.22(3.56)	2.03(4.44)
Post Secondary	2.48(5.78)	4.96(7.38)	0.88(3.63)	3.39(6.53)
vocational	0.07(0.25)	0.09(0.29)	0.04(0.20)	0.05(0.22)
Experience	21.8(12.5)	19.4(0.29)	23.1(12.4)	21.0(12.1)
Experience^2 $\times10^{-2}$	6.34(6.50)	5.14(5.71)	6.88(6.74)	5.87(6.26)
Age < 35	0.48 (0.50)	0.46 (0.50)	0.51(0.50)	0.51(0.50)
Age 35-44	0.24(0.43)	0.33(0.47)	0.24(0.43)	0.31(0.46)
Age 45-64	0.28(0.45)	0.21(0.41)	0.24(0.43)	0.18(0.38)
Primary4*Age35-44	0.014(0.24)	0.01(0.19)	0.036(0.38)	0(0)
Primary6*Age35-44	0.11(0.79)	0.09(0.75)	0.12(0.85)	0(0)
Primary8*Age35-44	0.028(0.47)	0.07(0.76)	0.017(0.37)	0(0)
Junior*Age35-44	0.27(1.53)	0.22(1.39)	0.19(1.29)	0.06(0.72)
Secondary*Age35-44	0.72(2.85)	1.31(1.39)	0.36(2.04)	0.81(3.02)

Post Sec*Age 35-44	0.65(3.15)	1.45(4.57)	0.22(1.88)	0.97(3.82)
Primary4*Age45-64	0.10(0.63)	0.036(0.38)	0.07(0.54)	0.05(0.45)
Primary6*Age45-64	0.066(0.62)	0.014(0.29)	0.08(0.68)	0.02(0.34)
Junior*Age45-64	0.28(1.55)	0.12(1.01)	0.16(1.19)	0.06(0.72)
Secondary*Age45-64	0.59(2.59)	0.57(2.56)	0.24(1.70)	0.35(2.02)
Post Sec*Age45-64	0.76(3.39)	0.72(3.29)	0.29(2.11)	0.36(2.36)
Experience*Age35-44	5.49(10.2)	7.03(10.7)	6.28(11.4)	7.72(12.2)
Experience*Age45-64	10.6(17.3)	7.30(14.9)	9.73(17.5)	6.90(15.3)
Experience^2*Age35-44	1.34(2.75)	1.65(2.91)	1.69(3.27)	2.07(3.63)
Experience^2*Age45-64	4.12(7.31)	2.74(6.15)	4.01(7.67)	2.80(6.70)
Rural		0((0.0)	1(0.0)	1(0)
Khartoum	0.20(0.40)	0.21(0.40)	0.03(0.18)	0.02(0.16)
Northern	0.11(0.31)	0.12(0.32)	0.20(0.40)	0.21(0.40)
Eastern	0.27(0.45)	0.18(0.39)	0.16(0.36)	0.09(0.29)
Central	0.22(0.42)	0.24(0.43)	0.38(0.48)	0.28(0.45)
Kordofan	0.08(0.27)	0.10(0.30)	0.11(0.31)	0.15(0.36)
Darfur	0.12(0.32)	0.15(0.35)	0.12(0.33)	0.25(0.43)
Married	0.62(0.49)	0.71(0.46)	0.68(0.46)	0.76(0.42)
Non Earned Household income	881.26(13536.4)	926.97(5512.54)	157.17(959.47)	280.48(1991.7)
Owned land	0.08(0.27)	0.07(0.26)	0.36(0.48)	0.43(0.49)
Rent Land	0.04(0.20)	0.034(0.18)	0.11(0.32)	0.16(0.37)
Partially Owned Land	0.01(0.10)	0.009(0.09)	0.02(0.13)	0.035(0.18)

Communal Land	0.007(0.08)	0.009(0.09)	0.03(0.17)	0.019(0.14)
Sample	2176		2657	

Note: standard deviations in parentheses.

Table A3: Ordinary Least Square Estimates of the wage Function (Dependent Variable Log Monthly Wage Rate)

Variable	Males		Females	
	Coefficient	t-ratio	Coefficient	t-ratio
(Constant)	5.16	56.7	4.69	19.9
Primary4	-0.031	-0.83	0.355	2.41
Primary6	0.019	1.49	0.066	1.91
Primary8	0.031	3.67	0.052	1.73
Junior Secondary	0.024	2.25	0.075	2.14
Secondary	0.043	8.85	0.082	6.87
Post-Secondary	0.048	10.7	0.071	7.62
vocational	0.138	2.47	0.205	1.78
Experience	0.046	4.05	0.033	1.18
Experience^2 $\times 10^{-2}$	-0.094	-2.37	-0.061	-0.63
Rural	-0.237	-8.81	-0.300	-4.56
Age 35-44	-0.240	-0.42	0.698	0.73
Age 45-64	-0.328	-0.54	2.41	1.29
Interaction Terms:				
Primary4*Age35-44	0.128	2.40	-0.741	-2.99
Primary6*Age35-44	0.021	1.04	-0.005	-0.07
Junior*Age35-44	0.006	0.39	-0.017	-0.37
Secondary*Age35-44	-0.001	-0.12	-0.029	-1.41
Post Sec*Age 35-44	0.005	0.50	-0.027	-1.41
Primary4*Age45-64	0.098	2.26	-0.267	-1.64

Primary6*Age45-64	0.065	2.77	-0.023	-0.22
Junior*Age45-64	0.021	1.46	-0.027	-0.49
Secondary*Age45-64	0.017	1.89	-0.038	-1.46
Post Sec*Age45-64	0.029	3.65	-0.033	-1.21
Experience*Age35-44	0.010	0.23	-0.029	-0.37
Experience*Age45-64	-0.006	-0.20	-0.089	-0.96
Experience^2*Age35-44	0.001	0.01	0.058	0.33
Experience^2*Age45-64	0.053	0.97	0.097	0.67
Regions:				
Northern	-0.321	-6.37	-0.089	-0.76
Eastern	-0.274	-5.77	-0.304	-2.65
Central	-0.248	-5.37	-0.316	-3.02
Kordofan	-0.369	-6.57	-0.399	-3.24
Darfur	-0.284	-5.38	-0.210	-1.83
Adjusted R^2	0.192		.294	
F(K,N-K)	32.23		11.05	
Sample	4084		749	

Table A4: Monthly Earning by Education, Location and Gender for the Subsample of Wage Earners in SDG:

	Urban		Rural	
	Males	females	Males	Females
no education	335.53	178.37	222.09	146.36
	(259.01)	(206.92)	(183.67)	(244.82)
	[280]	[150]	[200]	[100]
khalwa	309.53	223.33	276.69	247.5
	(194.57)	(302.81)	(224.65)	(387.74)
	280	[140]	[240]	[72.5]
incomplete primary	287.70	181.30	232.57	140.46
	(171.80)	(106.42)	(165.66)	(88.309)
	[280]	[150]	[205]	[125]
primary4	417.07	292	288	185.5
	(256.20)	(231.80)	(182.82)	(101.13)
	[350]	[232]	[280]	[186]
primary6	385.52	248.15	284.10	216.63
	(285.18)	(165.22)	(205.72)	(123.29)
	[300]	[210]	[210]	[195]
primary8	282.60	258.15	279.60	188
	(178.10)	(243.76)	(189.72)	(156.59)
	[280]	[196]	[240]	[120]
junior secondary	369.63	327.57	301.43	335.85
	(194.41)	(160.88)	(195.02)	(129.23)
	[330]	[312]	[265]	[365]

some/complete secondary	411.16	363.53	361.10	340.05
	(310.42)	(222.79)	(263.77)	(169.79)
	[350]	[300]	[300]	[300]
post-secondary	667.95	415.67	560.59	364.83
	(620.54)	(271.57)	(465.22)	(153.07)
	[500]	[380]	[450]	[350]

Table A5: Returns to investment in education by level (regional averages) (%):

Country	Social			Private		
	Primary	Secondary	Higher	Primary	Secondary	Higher
Sub-Saharan Africa	24.3	18.2	11.2	41.3	26.6	27.8
Asia	19.9	13.3	11.7	39.0	18.9	19.9
Europe/Middle East/North Africa	15.5	11.2	10.6	17.4	15.9	21.7
Latin America/ Caribbean	17.9	12.8	12.3	26.2	16.8	19.7
OECD	14.4	10.2	8.7	21.7	12.4	12.3
World	18.4	13.1	10.9	29.1	18.1	20.3

Source: Psacharopoulos (1994).

TableA6: Returns to investment in education by levels of education, averages by per capita income group (%)

Country	Mean per capita (US$)	Social			Private		
		Primary	Secondary	Higher	Primary	Secondary	Higher
Low income ($610 or less)	299	23.4	15.2	10.6	35.2	19.3	23.5
Lower middle income (to $2,449)	1,402	18.2	13.4	11.4	29.9	18.7	18.9
Upper middle income (to $7,619)	4,184	14.3	10.6	9.5	21.3	12.7	14.8
High income ($7,620)	13,100	n.a.	10.3	8.2	n.a.	12.8	7.7
World	2,020	20.0	13.5	10.7	30.7	17.7	19.0

Source: Psacharopoulos (1994).

Table A7: Returns to education by gender (%)

Educational level	Men	Women
Primary	20.1	12.8
Secondary	13.9	18.4
Higher	13.4	12.7
Overall	11.1	12.4

Source: Psacharopoulos (1994)

References:

Assad, R. (1997), "The Effects of Public Sector Hiring and Compensation Policies on the Egyptian Labor Market," The World Bank Economic Review, vol.11, no.1, pp. 85-118.

Becker, G. S (1964), Human Capital: A Theoretical and Empirical Analysis, with Special Reference to Education, New York: National Bureau of Economic Research.

-------------- (1962), "Investment in Human Capital: A Theoretical Analysis," Journal of Political Economy, Supplement, 70:5, Part 2, S9-S 49.

Bennell, P. (1996), "Rates of Return to Education: Does the Conventional Pattern Prevail in Sub-Saharan Africa". World Development Journal, vol.24, no.1.

Birdsall, N. (1985), "Public Inputs and Child Schooling in Brazil," Journal of Development Economics, vol. 18, pp. 67-86.

Clark, D. (2002), "The Impact of Labor Market Conditions on Participation in Further Education in England," IZA DP No. 550, Bonn: Germany.

Chernichovsky, D. (1985), "Socioeconomic and Demographic Aspects of School Enrollment and Attendance in Rural Botswana," Economic Development and Cultural Change, No. 2, pp. 319- 332.

Chiswick, B. R. (1997), "Interpreting the Coefficient of Schooling in Human Capital Earnings Function," Human Development Department, World Bank.

Cohen, B. and House, J. (1994), "Education, Experience and Earnings in the Labor   Market of a Developing Economy: The Case of Urban Khartoum". World Development Journal, vol.22, no.10, pp.1549-1994.

Doeringer, P. B. and Michael J. Piore (1980), "The Internal Labor Market," in King, J. E. (ed.), Readings in Labor Economics, Oxford: Oxford University Press.

Deaton and Muelbauer (1980), Consumer Behavior. Cambridge: Cambridge University Press.

Griliches, Z. (1977), "Estimating the Returns to Schooling: Some Econometric Problems," Econometrica, Vol. 45, No. 1, pp 1-22.

-------------- (1970), "Notes on the Role of Education in Production Functions and Growth Accounting," in W. Lee Hansen (ed.), Education, Income and Human Capital, New York: National Bureau of Economic Research.

Gronau, R. (1974), "The Effect of Children on the Housewife's Value of Time," In Economics of the Family, T. W.Schultz (ed.). New York: Columbia University Press.

Heckman, J. J. (1974), "Shadow Prices, Market Wages, and Labor Supply," Econometrica, Vol. 42, No. 4, pp. 679-694.

------------- (1979), "Sample Selection Bias as a Specification Error," Econometrica, vol. 47, pp.153-62.

------------- (1980), "Sample Selection Bias as Specification Error with an Application to the Estimation of Labor supply Functions," in Smith ed. (1980), pp.206-248.

Harmon, K. (2011), "Economic Returns to Education: What We Know, What We don't, and Where We are Going- Some pointers,' IZA Policy Paper No. 29, Bonn: Germany.

Kuru, J., Eldah Onsomu and Fredrick Wamalwa (2009), Education, Training and Youth Unemployment in Kenya," GDN Working Paper Series, Working Paper No. 26.

Kuna, E. N. A. (2003), Returns to Education in the Sudan, Unpublished Ph.D. thesis, Gezira University, Wadmedani, Sudan.

Khandker, S. R. (1989), "Returns to Schooling and Male-Female Wage Differences in Peru," PHRWD, The World Bank.

Jamison, D. T. and M. E. Lockheed (1987), "Participation in Schooling: Determinants and Learning Outcomes in Nepal, "Economic Development and Cultural Change", vol. 26, No.2, pp. 279-306.

Lane, J, G. Hakim and J. Miranda (1999), "Labor Market Analysis and Public Policy: The Case of Morocco," The World Bank Economic Review, Vol. 13, No. 3, pp 561- 78.

Leontaridi, R.L (1998), "Segmented labor Markets: Theory and Evidence", Journal of Economic Surveys, vol. 12, No 1, pp 63-101.

Mincer, J. (1974), Schooling, Experience and Earnings, New York: Columbia University Press.

----------- (1980),"Human Capital and Earnings," in A. B. Atkinson (ed.), Wealth, Income and Inequality, Oxford: Oxford University Press

Mincer, J. and S. Polachek (1974), "Family Investments in Human Capital: Earnings of women." in T. W. Schultz, ed. Economics of the Family: Marriage, Children and Human Capital, pp.397-429.New York: Columbia University Press.

Ministry of High Education and Scientific Research (MHESR), Annual Report; various issues, Khartoum, Sudan.

Maglad, N. (1994), "School Supply, Family Background and Gender- Specific School Enrollment and Attainment in Sudan," Eastern Africa Social Science Research Review, vol. x, No.2 (June).

Maglad, A.M. (1998), "Female Labor Supply in Sudan". African Economic Research Consortium, Special Paper No.30.

Oaxaca, R. (1973), "Male-Female Wage Differentials in Urban Labor Markets," International Economic Review, vol. 14 pp. 693 - 709.

Pastore, F. (2005), "To Study or To Work? Education and Labor Market Participation of Young People in Poland," IZA DP No. 1793, Bonn: Germany.

Psacharopoulos, G. (1981), "Returns to Education: An Updated International Comparison," Comparative Education, vol. 17, pp. 321-41.

------------------(1985), "Returns to Education: A Further International Update and Implications," Journal of Human Resources 20, pp. 583-604.

-------------------- (1994), "Returns to Investment in Education: A Global Update". World Development, vol.22, no.9, pp.1325-1343.

Stelcner, M., J. van der Gaag and W. Vijverberg (2001),"A Switching Regression Model of Public-Private Sector Wage Differentials in Peru: 1985-86," The Journal of Human Resources Vol.24, No.3, pp545-558.

Schultz, T. P (2003), "Evidence of Returns to Schooling in Africa from Household Surveys: Monitoring and Restructuring the Market for Education," Discussion Paper No. 875. New Haven, New Haven, CT: Economic Growth Center, Yale University.

----------------- (1992), "The role of Education and Human Capital in Economic Development: An Empirical Assessment," Discussion Paper No. 670. New Haven, CT: Economic Growth Center, Yale University.

-------------- (1990), "Returns to Women Education," Discussion Paper No. 603. New Haven, CT: Economic Growth Center, Yale University.

--------------(1988),"Educational Investment and Returns," In Handbook of Development Economics, vol. 1, H. Chenery and T. N. Srinivasan (eds.). Amsterdam: North Holland.

Schultz, T. W. (1961), "Investment in Human Capital," American Economic Review, 51, No 1, pp 1-17.

---------------- (1960), "Capital Formation by Education," Journal of Political Economy, Vol. 68, No 6, pp 571-583.

Singh, R. D. (1992), "Underinvestment, Low Economic Returns to Education and Schooling of Rural Children: Some Evidence from Brazil," Economic Development and Cultural Change, vol. 40, No. 3, pp. 654-664.

Tansel, A. (1994), "Wage Employment, Earnings and Returns to Schooling for Men and Women in Turkey". Economics of Education Review, vol.13, no.4, pp. 305-320.

Vijverberg, W.P.M (2001),"Educational Investments and Returns for Women and Men in Cote d'Ivoire," The Journal of Human Resources Vol. 28 No. 4, pp. 934-974.

Willis, R. J. (1986), "Wage Determinants: A survey and Reinterpretation of Human Capital Earnings Function," in O. Ashenfelter and R. Layard (eds.), Handbook of labor Economics, chapter 10. Amestrdam: Elsevier Science Publishers

Chapter Four

Labor Economic Efficiency in Agriculture

1. Introduction:

The purpose of this chapter is to compare the behavior of different groups of farms in rural Sudan using the profit function approach. First, we test whether small and large farms are equally efficient relatively. This is an important question which has been treated in the literature for some developing countries (Lau and Yotopoulos [1971] and Yotopoulos and Lau [1973], Junanker [1980a] and Khan *et al.* [1979] to mention a few).

The relative abundance of cultivable land in Sudan compared to other countries and the unique evolvement of land ownership which put much of the cultivable land under the Government control [Awad, 1971] may be one reason why the issue has been neglected. Today, the drought of the past decades and the vigorous Government policies to establish the vast rain land plains of the country along the large scale mechanized farms, have derived many of the small cultivators and nomadic tribes away from their lands. Some of these have settled in the irrigated state agricultural enterprises as laborers. For decades these schemes have been a magnet for people from the rain-fed sector, providing employment during the long periods of the dry season. Over the years some have acquired land and settled. This brings us to the second test which we shall examine: equal relative efficiency of farmers who were immigrant versus the local ones.

Thirdly, the Government policies regarding the development of the agricultural sector in the last decade has centered on the creation of incentives through the market system. The underlying assumption is, of course, that farmers are profit maximizers, who respond to the price signals according to the dictates of neoclassical economics. We shall be able to examine this assertion as we proceed with the data analysis. The remaining sections of this paper run as follows. The next section is devoted to the discussion of the data and the sample that will be used in the analysis. Also, the empirical specification of the functional form that will be adopted to test the advanced hypotheses is presented. Section 3 gives the empirical results and a conclusion is offered in Section 4.

2. Data and Empirical specification:

Data for the analysis are drawn from a stratified random sample of 599 agricultural households making their living in the Suki Scheme, and spread over 26 villages in the Scheme's area. The main crop which is cultivated by the farmers is cotton, and is grown in a tenancy size of five feddans for each farmer. Areas grown by households differ because some households are composed of more than one tenancy owner. Subsistence cultivation of the staple food crop `sorghum' is also practiced in some part of the land.

This paper is concerned with the economic efficiency of cotton cultivation, which is invariably the cash crop in all other state schemes like Suki, and the main export crop for the country. Usually, the Government provides the farmer with all the agricultural inputs used in cotton production (seeds, fertilizers, capital services, irrigation, etc.) on per feddan basis. Labor inputs and hiring of labor (usually during harvesting) is the farmer's responsibility. Only 334 households of the total sample has been used because in some observations part of the variables needed in the analysis, e.g. the wage rate, since not all households hire labor, are missing.

The development of the profit function approach to study differences in economic efficiency between different groups of farms has been carried out by Lau and Yotopoulos [1971] and Yotopoulos and Lau [1973]. Since then many applications have come out and a summary and assessment can be found in Junanker [1989]. Following the approach, an estimating stochastic profit and variable factor demand functions, to test for differences in economic efficiency between small and large farms, may be written respectively as:

$$\ln \Pi^* = \ln \overset{*}{A}{}^s + \delta^l D^l + \alpha^*{}_1 \ln W_s + \alpha^*{}_2 \ln W_b + \beta^* \ln H + \varepsilon_1 \qquad (1)$$

$$\frac{-W_s L_s}{\Pi^*} = \overset{*}{\alpha}{}^s{}_1 D^s + \overset{*}{\alpha}{}^l{}_2 D^l + \varepsilon_2 \qquad (2)$$

$$(A)$$

$$\frac{-W_b L_b}{\Pi^*} = \alpha^* {}^s{}_2 D^s + \alpha^* {}^l{}_2 D^l + \varepsilon_3 \qquad (3)$$

Where

Π^* :Normalized or real profit in pounds and is equal to total revenue from cotton output minus total variable costs (equal to total labor costs in our case) normalized by the unit price of output.

153

L_s: Quantity of labor (Mandays) used in land preparation, planting and weeding and is referred to as slack season labor.

L_b: Quantity of labor (Mandays) used in harvesting and is busy season labor.

W_s: Real wage rate for labor in slack season. This is calculated by dividing the sum of wages paid to hired labor and imputed family labor (valued at the wage paid to hired labor) by the total labor of hired and family workers and then dividing by the unit price of output.

W_b: Real wage rate for labor in busy season. It is equal to the sum of total wages paid to hired and imputed family labor in harvesting divided by the total Mandays of family and hired labor in that season and then dividing by output price.

H: Total land cultivated in feddans.

D^l: Size dummy for large farms: equal 1 for farms of size larger than 5 feddans and zero otherwise.

D^s: Size dummy for small farms: Equal 1 for farms with area equal to or less than 5 feddans and zero otherwise.

$\varepsilon_1, \varepsilon_2, \varepsilon_3$: Stochastic error terms.

The profit function relationship in (1) assumes that the underlying production function is of the Cobb-Douglas type. Two variable inputs and one fixed inputs are presumed in the formulation in (1). These are respectively slack season labor Ls, busy season labor Lb and land cultivated H. It is hoped by introducing these two types of labor to capture, to some extent, the sequential decisions in the agricultural production process and to distinguish roughly between different types of labor (family versus hired) since hired labor is used mostly during the busy (harvesting) season and family labor is used in both slack and busy season. Using Hotteling's lemma, the variable inputs demand functions for slack labor L_s and busy labor $L_b.$, can be shown to be derived by differentiating the profit function equation in (1) with respect to their respective prices W_s and W_b . No measure of capital is included in (1) since all capital requirements (irrigation, tractors, etc.) are owned by the Government which provides capital services (including seeds, fertilizers) on per feddan basis. The capital expenditure by each farmer is thus highly correlated with the amount of land cultivated.

The set of equations in (A) will be used to test if there is equal relative economic efficiency between small and large farms. Economic efficiency implies both technical efficiency (ability to obtain the highest output from a given set of inputs) and price or allocative efficiency (equating the marginal value productivity of a factor to its price). If the two groups of farms are relatively equal economically in terms of efficiency, we expect that the profit functions of small and large farms to coincide with each other, i.e. the coefficient of the dummy Dl differentiating between the two groups of farms is zero. So the first hypothesis to test is:

$$H_0 : \delta^l = 0 \qquad \qquad (i)$$

However, because economic efficiency implies both price and technical efficiency, two groups of farms may be equally efficient economically without being equally price efficient or equally efficient technically. In order to make the latter distinction use is made of the factor demand functions in (2) and (3). A test of equal relative price efficiency will consist of testing whether the factor shares in equations (2) and (3) are equal for small and large farms, i.e.

$$H_0 : \overset{*s}{\alpha}_1 = \overset{*l}{\alpha}_1 \text{ and } \overset{*s}{\alpha}_2 = \overset{*l}{\alpha}_2 \qquad \qquad (ii)$$

A test of equal relative technical and price efficiency of the two groups consists of examining the hypothesis

$$H_0 : \delta^l = 0 , \overset{*s}{\alpha}_1 = \overset{*l}{\alpha}_1 \text{ and } \overset{*s}{\alpha}_2 = \overset{*l}{\alpha}_2 \qquad \qquad (iii)$$

Finally, the hypothesis of absolute price efficiency, i.e. whether a group of firms have maximized profits subject to given prices, will be investigated. This consists of testing the validity of parametric constraints across profit and factor share equations for each group of firms, namely

$$H_0 : \overset{*s}{\alpha}_1 = \alpha^*_1 \text{ and } \overset{*s}{\alpha}_2 = \alpha^*_2 \qquad \qquad (iv)$$
$$H_0 : \overset{*l}{\alpha}_1 = \alpha^*_1 \text{ and } \overset{*l}{\alpha}_2 = \alpha^*_2 \qquad \qquad (v)$$

A set of equations similar to the ones in (A) is estimated to test differences of economic efficiency between groups of immigrant tenants and local population. These may be written as follows:

$$\ln \Pi^* = \ln \overset{*n}{A} + \delta^m D^m + \alpha^*_1 \ln W_s + \alpha^*_2 \ln W_b + \beta^* \ln H + \varepsilon_1 \quad (4)$$

$$\frac{-W_s L_s}{\Pi^*} = \overset{*n}{\alpha}_1 D^n + \overset{*m}{\alpha}_1 D^m + \varepsilon_2 \qquad \qquad (5)$$

$$(B)$$

$$\frac{-W_b L_b}{\Pi^*} = \overset{*}{\alpha}n \,_2 D^n + \overset{*}{\alpha}m \,_2 D^m + \varepsilon_3 \qquad\qquad (6)$$

Tests corresponding to the ones in (i), (ii), (iii), (iv) and (v) are carried in this case for groups' n (non-migrants) and m (migrants).

Choice of the Cobb-Douglas production function, and hence a Cobb-Douglas profit function, was not dictated by any a priori reasons except easiness of estimation. However, because of the restrictive nature of the Cobb-Douglas production function (unit elasticity of substitution) and the restrictive implications of its dual, the profit function [Chand and Kaul, 1986] a general trans-log functional form will be fitted to test whether the chosen specification is right. With two variable inputs, Ls and L_b and one fixed input H , the translog profit function is written as

$$\ln \Pi^* = \alpha_0 + \alpha_1 \ln W_s + \alpha_2 \ln W_b + \tfrac{1}{2}\, \gamma_{11}(\ln W_s)^2$$
$$+ \tfrac{1}{2}\, \gamma_{12} \ln W_s \ln W_b + \tfrac{1}{2}\gamma_{22}(\ln W_b)^2 + \delta_{1h} \ln W_s \ln H$$
$$+ \delta_{2h} \ln W_b \ln W_s \ln H + \beta \ln H \qquad\qquad (7)$$

Where the variables are as defined before. Differentiating the translog profit function with respect to ln W_i (i = s,b) gives a system of variable input/profit ratio functions [Diewert, 1974]. For the profit function to be Cobb-Douglas, coefficients of all second-order terms in (7) should be zero. Thus, a test will be conducted of the null hypothesis:

$$H_0 : \gamma_{ij} = 0 \ \forall i, j \ \text{and} \ \delta_{ih} = 0 , \ i = 1, 2 \qquad\qquad (vi)$$

The random error terms in each of the equations in model (A) and model (B) are assumed to have zero mean and constant variance. However, the covariance of the errors across a pair of equations is assumed to be non-zero. Thus the models were estimated using Zellner's Seemingly Unrelated Regressions which gives asymptotically efficient estimates. The following section discusses the estimates of the profit function and the results of the hypotheses' tests.

3. RESULTS

The estimated parameters of the model in (A) are provided in Table 1.A and the parallel estimates of model (B) are given in Table 1.B. The first two lines in the tables give respectively the unrestricted Ordinary Least Squares (OLS) estimates and Zellner's Seemingly Unrelated Regression (SUR) estimates of the profit and demand functions. Lines (3)-(7) gives the restricted estimates using SUR and the corresponding χ^2-statistics computed to test for these restrictions are provided in Table 2.

From Table 1.A we note that the size dummy for large farms turns out with a negative sign in the profit equation in all the cases. This would seem to suggest that small farms have an advantage over large ones. However, the difference is not statistically significant at 5% level of significance. In the labor demand functions equations the small size dummy is highly statistically significant in almost all the cases while the large size dummy is not statistically significant in most of the cases (significant under the restrictions $\alpha = \alpha$, which is rejected) and especially so for the slack labor demand function. Turning to the tests of differences in economic efficiency we see from Table 2, from the computed χ^2-statistics, that the hypothesis that there is no difference in economic efficiency between small and large farms cannot be rejected at 5% level of significance. Moreover, the computed statistics in (ii) and (iii) in the Table means that the hypothesis that the two groups are also equally technical and price efficient cannot be rejected.

Table 1.B, on the other hand, shows that groupings of farms on the basis of migrant (m) and non-migrant (n) category gives different implications regarding economic efficiency. We observe that the coefficient on the migrant group dummy in the profit function is always positive and significantly different from zero at 5% level of significance. The $\chi 2$ test in Table 2, part (B), shows that the migrant groups are indeed superior on economic efficiency grounds as the hypothesis that $\delta m = 0$ cannot be accepted at 5% level of significance and whether this difference can be attributed to differences in allocation or technical efficiency can be read from the tests provided in B (ii)-(iii) in Table 2. The computed $\chi 2$ in B (ii) to test for differences on price-efficiency indicates that the hypothesis of equal price efficiency cannot be rejected at 5% significance level. Also, the $\chi 2$ test in B (iii) (Table 2) shows that the hypothesis of equal relative technical and price efficiency for the two groups is rejected. Thus the difference in economic efficiency between the two groups is related to differences on technical efficiency grounds, on which the migrants are superior. This difference could be the result of the superior quality or intensity of labor used by the immigrant groups, a thing which is well observed in many of the development schemes like the Suki.

Having said that, it is important to note that, as obvious from testing hypotheses (iv) and (v) (very high computed value of $\chi 2$ in Table 2), none of the groups (small/large and migrant/non-migrant) is absolutely price efficient. This means that a necessary and sufficient condition test of profit maximization is rejected. In fact, looking back at Table 1.A and/or Table 1.B, we observe that one of the price variables, Wb, turned out with a wrong sign ($\alpha_2 > 0$) and is always statistically significant. And when the other price variable Ws has the right sign ($\alpha_1 < 0$) it is not statistically significant in any of the cases. Land always has the right sign but the coefficient attached to it is very high. This may be because land is capturing the effect of fixed variables not included in the regression that are highly correlated with it, viz. capital. In fact a test of the hypothesis that $\beta = 1$ (constant returns to scale) is rejected as one should expect (not reported).

Many reasons could be offered for the observed behavior of the estimated parameters in a profit function approach in the analysis of data from low-income country agricultural sector (Junanker [1980a, 1980b and 1989] for a discussion). The possibility that the functional form of the profit function is misspecified is investigated by estimating a more general form, namely, the translog form, of which the Cob-Douglas is a special case. A test of the hypothesis that the true functional form is a Cobb-Douglas when the estimated function is translog is performed. The computed χ^2-statistics when the restrictions in (vi) are imposed on equation (7) turned at 15.68, higher than the critical value of χ_{05} at 8 degrees of freedom, which is equal to 15.51. Thus the data reject the Cobb-Douglas profit (and hence production) function specification. The Appendix provides the estimates of the translog profit function and the factor demands based on it.

4. **Concluding Remarks:**

This chapter examined the differences in economic efficiency between small and large farms, using micro-level data from the irrigated cotton producing sector of the Sudanese economy. This issue has not been given the attention it deserves since abundance of cultivable lands and the development of irrigated schemes, in which farmers were given tenure to sufficiently equal land plots, have not led to questions of equity and land distribution being of prominent importance at the initial stages of agricultural development in the Sudan.

However, the continuous Government policy of extensive cultivation, particularly of the cash crops and capitalist large scale farming in the rain-fed sector, has pushed the cultivable margin to its limits and pressure on cultivable land has begun to be felt. Many of the rural populace in the latter sector who has been engaged in traditional cultivation of communally owned and private lands has joined the ranks of their predecessors as landless labor in the irrigated schemes, like Gezira, ElRahad and Es Suki.

The empirical results of the study teach us two lessons. There is no economic advantage of large farms over small ones. On the contrary, small farms seem to have a marginal advantage in the used data set. Also, the migrant population which has for long provided the labor force for cotton harvesting in the irrigated sector appears to be economically superior on technical grounds but as price efficient as the rest of the population. Secondly, there is no support from the data analyzed for the contention that the cotton cultivators are profit maximizers.

REFERENCES

Awad, M. H., 1971, "The Evolution of Land Ownership in Sudan," Middle East Journal, Vol. 25, No. 2.

Chand R, and J.L. Kaul, 1986, "A Note on the Use of the Cobb-Douglas Profit Function." American Journal of Agricultural Economics, Vol. 68, No. 1, pp. 162-4.

Diewert, W. E., 1974, "Applications of Duality Theory," in Frontiers in Quantitative Economics, Vol. 11, edited by M. D. Intriligator and D. A. Kendrick. Amsterdam: North-Holland.

Junanker, P. N., 1980a, "Tests of Profit Maximization Hypothesis: A Study of Indian Agriculture," Journal of Development Studies, Vol. 6, No. 6, pp. 186-203.

_____, 1980b, "Do Indian Farmers Maximize Profits," Journal of Development Studies, Vol. 17, No. 1, pp. 48-61.

_____, 1989, "The Response of Peasant Farmers to Price Incentives: The Use and Misuse of Profit Functions," Journal of Development Studies, Vol. 25, No. 2, pp. 169-182.

Khan, M. H. and D. R. Maki, 1979, "Effects of Farm Size and Economic Efficiency: The Case of Pakistan," American Journal of Agricultural Economics, Vol. 61, No. 1, pp. 64-69.

Lau, L. I. and P. A. Yotopoulos, 1971, "A Test for Relative Efficiency and Application of Indian Agriculture," American Economic Review, Vol. 61, No. 1, pp. 94-109.

Yotopoulos, P. A. and L. I. Lau, 1973, "A Test for Relative Economic Efficiency: Some Further Results," American Economic Review, Vol. 63, No. 1, pp. 214-223.

Table 1.A
Cobb-Douglas Profit Function and Labor Demand Functions

No.	Estimation Method	Restriction	Constant	δ^l	Profit Function Equation α^*_1	α^*_2	B^*
1.	OLS	None	-.633	-.507	-.166	.344	2.139
			(-.666)	(-1.09)	(-1.86)	(4.51)	(4.10)
2.	Zellner	None	-.00621	-.447	-.043	.338	2.032
			(.008)	(-1.12)	(-.57)	(5.27)	(4.64)
3.	Zellner	$\delta^l = 0$	-.655	0	-.0432	.329	1.59
			(1.19)		(-.57)	(5.17)	(8.31)
4.	Zellner	$\alpha^{*s}_1 = \alpha^{*l}_1$	.0232	-.539	-.043	.339	2.032
		$\alpha^{*s}_2 = \alpha^{*l}_2$	(.03)	(-1.38)	(-.57)	(5.27)	(4.64)
5.	Zellner	$\delta^l = 0$	.852	0	-.043	.327	1.373
		$\alpha^{*s}_1 = \alpha^{*l}_1$	(1.61)		(-.58)	(5.14)	(8.76)
		$\alpha^{*s}_2 = \alpha^{*l}_2$					
6.	Zellner	$\alpha^{*s}_1 = \alpha^{*l}_1$	-.789	-.459	-.015	.085	1.99
		$\alpha^{*s}_2 = \alpha^{*l}_2$	(-.99)	(-1.15)	(-.22)	(1.91)	(4.56)
7.	Zellner	$\alpha^{*s}_1 = \alpha^{*l}_1$	-.245	-.218	-.00349	.244	2.016
		$\alpha^{*s}_2 = \alpha^{*l}_2$	(-.31)	(-.56)	(-.05)	(4.27)	(4.60)

Table 1.A (continued)

Estimation				Slack Labor Demand		Busy Labor Demand	
No.	Method	Restriction	Constant	α^{*s}_1	α^{*l}_1	α^{*s}_2	α^{*l}_2
1.	OLS	None	-.633	-.839	-.367	-.355	-.226
			(-.666)	(-4.24)	(-.88)	(-4.57)	(-1.38)
2.	Zellner	None	-.00621	-.839	-.368	-.355	-.226
			(.008)	(-4.26)	(-.89)	(-4.58)	(-1.39)
3.	Zellner	$\delta^l = 0$	-.655	-.859	-.281	-.363	-.194
			(1.19)	(-4.38)	(-.69)	(-4.69)	(-1.21)
4.	Zellner	$\alpha^{*s}_1 = \alpha^{*l}_1$	.0232	-.752	-.752	-.331	-.331
		$\alpha^{*s}_2 = \alpha^{*l}_2$	(.03)	(-4.23)	(4.23)	(-4.74)	(-4.74)
5.	Zellner	$\delta^l = 0$	.852	-.752	-.752	-.331	-.331
		$\alpha^{*s}_1 = \alpha^{*l}_1$	(1.61)	(-4.23)	(-4.23)	(-4.74)	(-4.74)
		$\alpha^{*s}_2 = \alpha^{*l}_2$					
6.	Zellner	$\alpha^{*s}_1 = \alpha^{*l}_1$	-.789	-.015	-.368	.085	-.226
		$\alpha^{*s}_2 = \alpha^{*l}_2$	(-.99)	(-.22)	(-.89)	(1.91)	(-1.39)
7.	Zellner	$\alpha^{*s}_1 = \alpha^{*l}_1$	-.245	-.839	-.00349	-.355	.244
		$\alpha^{*s}_2 = \alpha^{*l}_2$	(-.31)	(-4.26)	(-.05)	(-4.58)	(1.27)

Note: The estimated parameters correspond to the model in (A). Figures in parentheses are t-statistics.

Table 1.B
Cobb-Douglas Profit Function and Labor Demand Functions

Estimation No.	Method	Restriction	Constant	Profit Function Equation δ^m	α^*_1	α^*_2	B^*
1.	OLS	None	.019	.505	-.113	.312	1.636
			(.03)	(3.76)	(-1.27)	(4.18)	(8.32)
2.	Zellner	None	.694	.528	-.000477	.309	1.495
			(1.33)	(3.97)	(-.01)	(4.94)	(9.04)
3.	Zellner	$\delta^m = 0$	.849	0	-.0412	.326	1.478
			(1.63)		(-.56)	(5.21)	(8.94)
4.	Zellner	$\alpha^*n_1 = \alpha^{*m}_1$ $\alpha^*n_2 = \alpha^{*m}_2$	.735 (1.41)	.426 (3.77)	-.000477 (-.01)	.309 (4.94)	1.495 (9.04)
5.	Zellner	$\delta^m = 0$ $\alpha^*n_1 = \alpha^{*m}_1$ $\alpha^*n_2 = \alpha^{*m}_2$	.842	0	-.0461	.328	1.476
6.	Zellner	$\alpha^*n_1 = \alpha^*_1$ $\alpha^*n_2 = \alpha^*_2$	-.106 (-.21)	.301 (2.41)	.00905 (.13)	.123 (2.62)	1.629 (9.96)
7.	Zellner	$\alpha^*n_1 = \alpha^*_1$ $\alpha^*n_2 = \alpha^*_2$	.0428 (.09)	.709 (5.97)	.0594 (.85)	.153 (3.01)	1.59 (9.72)

Table 1.B (continued)

No.	Method	Restriction	Constant	Slack Labor Demand α^{*n}_1	Slack Labor Demand α^{*m}_1	Busy Labor Demand α^{*n}_2	Busy Labor Demand α^{*m}_2
1.	OLS	None	.019 (.03)	-.997 (-4.33)	-.386 (-1.37)	-.376 (-4.14)	-.265 (-2.39)
2.	Zellner	None	.694 (1.33)	-.997 (-4.35)	-.386 (1.38)	-.376 (-4.15)	-.265 (-2.40)
3.	Zellner	$\delta^m = 0$	.849 (1.63)	-.717 (-3.28)	-.805 (-3.10)	-.273 (-3.15)	-.419 (-4.05)
4.	Zellner	$\alpha^{*n}_1 = \alpha^{*m}_1$ $\alpha^{*n}_2 = \alpha^{*m}_2$	.735 (1.41)	-.752 (-4.24)	-.752 (-4.24)	-.331 (-4.74)	-.331 (-4.74)
5.	Zellner	$\delta^m = 0$ $\alpha^{*n}_1 = \alpha^{*m}_1$ $\alpha^{*n}_2 = \alpha^{*m}_2$	.842 (1.62)	-.752 (-4.24)	-.752 (-4.24)	-.331 (-4.74)	-.331 (-4.74)
6.	Zellner	$\alpha^{*n}_1 = \alpha^{*}_1$ $\alpha^{*n}_2 = \alpha^{*}_2$	-.106 (-.21)	.00905 (.13)	-.386 (-1.38)	.123 (2.62)	-.265 (-2.40)
7.	Zellner	$\alpha^{*m}_1 = \alpha^{*}_1$ $\alpha^{*m}_2 = \alpha^{*}_2$	.0428 (.09)	-.997 (-4.35)	.0594 (.85)	-.376 (-4.15)	.153 (3.01)

Note: The estimated parameters correspond to the model in (A). Figures in parentheses are t-statistics.

Table 2
Statistical Hypotheses Tested

Tested Hypothesis H_0	Computed χ^2
(A) (i) $\delta^l = 0$	1.25
(ii) $\alpha^{*s}_1 = \alpha^{*l}_1$, $\alpha^{*s}_2 = \alpha^{*l}_2$	1.08
(iii) $\delta^l = 0$, $\alpha^{*s}_1 = \alpha^{*l}_1$, $\alpha^{*s}_2 = \alpha^{*l}_2$	2.99
(iv) $\alpha^{*s}_1 = \alpha^*_1$, $\alpha^{*s}_2 = \alpha^*_2$	49.25*
(v) $\alpha^{*l}_1 = \alpha^*_1$, $\alpha^{*l}_2 = \alpha^*_2$	11.52*
(B) (i) $\delta^m = 0$	15.76*
(iii) $\delta^m = 0$, $\alpha^{*n}_1 = \alpha^{*m}_1$, $\alpha^{*n}_2 = \alpha^{*m}_2$	17.16*
(iv) $\alpha^{*n}_1 = \alpha^*_1$, $\alpha^{*n}_2 = \alpha^*_2$	41.71*
(v) $\alpha^{*m}_1 = \alpha^*_1$, $\alpha^{*m}_2 = \alpha^*_2$	21.17*

Note: *significantly different from zero at 5% significance level.

APPENDIX: Estimates of the Translog Profit Function and Labor Demand Functions

Variable	Profit Function Coefficient	Estimate
Constant	α_0	-.720 (3.08)
$\ln w_s$	α_1	-.886 (-1.14)
$\ln w_b$	α_2	.619 (.86)
$\frac{1}{2}(\ln w_s)$	γ_{11}	.0893 (.87)
$\frac{1}{2}\ln w_s \ln w_b$	γ_{12}	-.226 (-1.49)
$\frac{1}{2}(\ln w_b)^2$	γ_{22}	.0535 (.67)
$\ln w_s \ln H$	δ_{1h}	.324 (1.33)
$\ln w_b \ln H$	δ_{2h}	-.264 (-1.34)
$\ln H$	β	1.739 (1.60)

		Slack Labor Demand		Busy Labor Demand
Constant	α_1	-2.399 (-1.44)	α_2	-2.387 (-3.64)
$\ln w_s$	γ_{11}	-.689 (-2.91)	γ_{21}	-.148 (-1.59)
$\ln w_b$	γ_{12}	.420 (2.09)	γ_{22}	-.193 (-2.65)
$\ln H$	δ_{1h}	.455 (.85)	δ_{2h}	.339 (1.62)

Note: Parentheses contain t-statistics

Chapter 5
Migration Out of Agriculture:
Analysis Based on Village Data

1. Introduction:

The issue of rural-urban migration has been discussed widely in the literature of economic development. A number of papers have been devoted to the formulation of theoretical models for explaining the phenomenon and efforts were spent on the empirical testing of these models[1]. Most important the studies indicated the importance of education in migration decisions, since the educated are most likely to benefit by maximizing the future returns gained through higher incomes from employment in urban areas compared with what they expect to earn by staying in their villages. Employment opportunities in the village are also linked to the household ownership of land as the main asset from which income is generated and therefore it is expected that those coming from households with small land holding are more likely to migrate. Nonetheless, individuals coming from households with large ownership of land may be encouraged to attain higher education levels and be availed with the required financial resources to fund their migration to urban areas. Since migrants coming from poorer households are probably less educated than those coming from rich ones and may expect to hold low-paid jobs and be temporary unemployed they might be discouraged from leaving.

In this chapter the impact of education on the probability to migrate from rural to urban areas, and the differential impact of education for different socio-economic groups is examined. The influence of land ownership and how it is related to the migration decision and impact of off-farm income will be examined. The remaining sections of the chapter are organized as follows. Section 2 reviews the economic hypotheses and in section 3 the data and the empirical specification are discussed. Section 4 presents the result and a summary is offered in section 5.

2. Economic Hypothesis:

The literature on rural-urban migration abounds with the push-pull factors behind the phenomenon. The low job opportunities and hence low expected levels of income and remuneration tend to push persons to leave their rural dwellings and toward the cities, where modern industrial and informal urban services and trade sectors offer a higher expected level of earnings. The underlying presumption is a utility or income maximizing individual who aims at optimizing the net gains from migrating to the urban centers.

Thus, an individual faced at time t with an average income of the employed being $Y_u(t)$ and $Y_r(t)$, in the urban and rural areas respectively, and where the probability of being employed in the urban area is $P_u(t)$, and in rural areas is one (i.e. no unemployment), would migrate if the present discounted values $V(0)$, of the difference between the stream of benefits in the source and receiving areas over his lifetime T, exceeds the costs of migration $C(0)$ (money and non-money)[2]. Thus, where

$$V(0) = \sum_{t=1}^{t=T} Pu\,(t)Yu\,(t) - Yr\,(t)/(1+i)t \qquad (1)$$

The decision to migrate will depend on whether or not

$$V\,(0) - C\,(0) \quad > \quad 0 \qquad\qquad\qquad (2)$$

A migration function Z can then be expressed as

$$Z = f\,(V\,(0), H) \qquad\qquad\qquad (3)$$

H is a vector of the individuals' characteristics that influence the decision to migrate. And, if migration decision is considered over a one period horizon, (3) can be expressed as

$$Z = f(Y_{eu} - Y_r, H) \qquad\qquad\qquad (4)$$

Y_{eu} is the expected urban income.

In Harris-Todaro model[3], migration is assumed to depend primarily on the expected rural-urban wage differential, where the probability of finding an urban job is expressed as the urban employment rate. Thus, it is implicitly assumed that the probability of finding an urban job is the same for everyone in the urban area labor force. Migration will continue as long as $Y_{eu} > Y_r$ and will stop when migration, through unemployment in the urban areas, has driven urban income to equality with rural income. The model has been criticized, mainly, in that it predicts higher than the actual unemployment rates. This stems from the specification of the probability of finding an urban job and the assumption that labor is employed in only the organized or formal markets[4].

In the next section, a migration response function is presented of the characteristics that influence the individual to take advantage of the employment opportunities by migrating to urban regions.

3. Data and Empirical Specification

The analysis of the determinants of rural-urban migration, and its impact on rural source areas is based on random samples of households from two villages: a Gezira village and a village from the Northern Province. The Gezira village, Wad Eljatra, is located in the northern part of the Gezira Scheme and the population of the village is engaged in the irrigated agriculture of cotton and staple food crops under the Scheme's management. The Northern Province village on the other hand is situated in Argou Island along the River Nile and the population earns its living by the cultivation of small plots of lands which are privately owned and irrigated by pumps either from the Nile or from artisan wells.

A total of 150 households in each village are selected, and household heads were interviewed on the socioeconomic characteristics of the unit. A total number of 71 families in Gezira village (47% of total) reported at least on migrant; the total number of migrants amounting to 81 giving an average number of migrants per migrant family of 1.14. In the Northern village households with at least one migrant amounted to 69 (46% of the total); with a total of 136 migrant the average migrant per migrant family is thus 1.97, almost twice the average for Gezira. In the analysis of migration decision the unit of observation shall be the adult persons ever present in the 300 households.

The migration function which is estimated is assumed to depend on the individual's age, sex, education level, farm-income, non-farm income and agricultural land owned. Farm Income, non-farm income and land are measured per adult in the household. Education is taken as a proxy for income earnings in urban areas and farm and non-farm income reflect the income opportunities at source areas. Table (1) gives the definition of variables, their means and standard deviations for a total of 1498 individuals, age 15 years and more, in the 300 households. Of the total sample 217 individuals were migrants, giving a migration probability of 0.15. Out of the 1498 individuals, 47% (703 individuals) belong to the households in the Gezira village and the rest come from Northern village households. The migrants' proportion is 0.12 and 0.17 in Gezira village and Northern village, respectively. International migration represents the bulk of migration, where 10% of the 15% are international migrants, the majority working in Saudi Arabia. 54% of the individuals in the sample are male and the average age is 33 years. More than a third of the individuals (36%) have no education at all. The percentage of individuals with at least primary level of education is higher in the Northern village compared with Gezira village; 70% of the individuals in the former have some education compared with 54% in the latter. The average landholding per adult is higher for Gezira compared with Northern area[5].

Table (1) Definition of Variables and Means (Standard Deviation)

Variable	Definition	All Sample	Gezira	Northern
Migrant	Dummy = 1 if an individual is migrant	.146 (0.35)	.120 (0.32)	.171 (0.37)
Age	Age of an Individual in years	32.9 (15.2)	32.9 (15.9)	32.9 (14.6)
Sex	Dummy = 1 if individual is male	.540 (0.58)	.548 (0.50)	.532 (0.64)
Education				
Primary	Dummy = 1 if education is primary	.241 (0.43)	.215 (0.41)	.264 (0.44)
Junior Secondary	Dummy = 1 if education is junior secondary	.198 (0.40)	.182 (0.39)	.211 (0.41)
High Secondary	Dummy = 1 if education is high secondary	.179 (0.38)	.144 (0.35)	.2101 (0.41)
Tertiary	Dummy = 1 if education is	.020	.016	.024

	tertiary	(0.14)	(0.12)	(0.15)

<u>Rural Income</u>

Farm Income per Adult	Total Value of Farm Output divided by Adults, 15 years and over, in household	583. (877.)	560. (495.)	603. (1110.)
Non - Farm income per Adult	Income from Off-Farm work divided by adults, 15 years and over, in household	333. (906.)	241. (453.)	413. (1163.)
Land-owned per adult	Area of land owned by household divided by adults, 15 years and over	2.59 (5.11)	2.89 (2.24)	2.32 (6.69)
Regional Dummy	Dummy = 1 if individual from Gezira	.469 (0.50)	1.00 (0.00)	.000 (0.00)
Sample Size		**1498**	**703**	**795**

4.Specification and Estimation:

It is hypothesized that the ith individual migration probability Z_i is a linear approximation of the explanatory variables x_j's

$$Z_i = \Sigma_j \, \beta_j \, x_{ij} \qquad\qquad (5)$$

And that an individual's choice regarding whether to stay in the rural area or move to an urban area is assumed to be made according to an unobserved function M^*, which is determined by the x_j's, and a random error u_i that is normally distributed, where

$$M^*_i = \Sigma_j \, \beta_j \, x_{ij} + u_i \qquad\qquad (6)$$

What is observed, however is dummy variable M_i, which takes the value 1 if an individual is a migrant and zero otherwise, that is

$$M_i = 1 \quad \text{if } M^*_i > 0$$
$$ = 0 \quad \text{otherwise} \tag{7}$$

From (6) and (7) we get

$$P_i = \text{Prob}(M_i=1) = \text{Prob}(\, u_i > -\Sigma \, \beta_j \, x_{ij} \,) = 1 - F(-Z) = F(Z) \tag{8}$$

F is the cumulative distribution of u. The likelihood function is then defined as

$$L = \Pi_{\, m=1} \, P_i \, \Pi_{\, m=0} \, (1 - P_i) \tag{9}$$

The assumption that the errors, u_i, are normally distributed gives a probit model, and the parameters are estimated by maximization of the likelihood function in (9)[6].

Regression Results:

The results of the estimated response function are presented in Table (2). The table provides the response coefficient for each explanatory variable and also the marginal effect of a change in that variable on the Prob (M=1)[7]. As the estimates show, all variables have the expected sign, and most of them significantly influence migration decision. The chi-squared statistics implies that all of the variables in the regression significantly influence the migration decision, and the value of R^2 shows that they explain a large portion of the variance in the dependent variable.

The likelihood to migrate is higher if the individual is a male and the migration function is related to age in quadratic form, with the probability of migration increasing in age until age 41 after which it declines. This association is noted in all migration studies. The justification for a non- linear relationship between migration and age is that migrants tend to maximize the expected discounted net returns by migrating while they are still young and as they become older loose the incentive to migrate[8].

The migration function is positively and significantly related to education for all education levels. The probability of migration is higher for those with a university level of education than for any of the other groups, and higher for those with a secondary education compared with those with primary level. Note that the effect of the junior secondary education level is higher than the higher secondary education level, suggesting that a higher proportion of the individuals with junior education level are migrants than those with higher secondary education. Some of the latter probably had remained at school and continued education beyond the junior secondary level. Thus, it seems that migration from the village starts mostly after an individual has finished the junior secondary level of education (when he is 16 years old).

Agricultural income, non-farm income and land ownership are all inversely related to migration decision but only agricultural income is significantly related to the migration decision. Agriculture is, of course, the main source of employment and income for the households in the sample. The effect of land is obviously underestimated because agricultural income and land are positively correlated.

The interaction terms are introduced in the regression to measure the differential impact of education on the migration probability for different landownership. The interaction between education and land ownership indicates that highly educated individuals coming from households with more land had a high propensity to migrate. With imperfect capital markets, households with large assets would be more capable than poor ones of providing the required fund for educating their children, and later in facilitating their migration and job search in urban areas. If these children hold high-salaried jobs, as is most probable, they would probably remit money back home, which might lead to an increase in income inequality at the source areas if migration has not spread sufficiently across the different income groups in the village. This suggestion needs to be examined using a decomposition of income inequality.

The marginal effects for the total sample in Table (2) indicate that education increases the probability to migrate by 9%-16%. The marginal effect of income shows the percentage decline in the probability to migrate for a unit (100 pounds) increase in income. Thus, an increase in per capita income by thousand pounds, that is almost double the sample mean income, would decrease the migration probability by 7%.

There seems to be no significant difference in the propensity to migrate between the two regions, though the probability to migrate appears to be lower in the Gezira village. Separate estimates of the migration function are carried out for each of the regions as shown in Table (2). There are a number of differences in the estimates of the coefficients between the two regions. Firstly, education is much more significant in explaining the migration decision in the Northern village than in Gezira. In fact it is noted that the university level of education is significant only in the Northern village. This is expected since there are more individuals with this level of education in the Northern village. Secondly, unlike the Northern village, non-farm income is significantly associated inversely with migration in the Gezira village. The opportunities for non-farm employment are in fact much larger in the Gezira than in the Northern villages.

Thirdly, regarding the interaction terms between education and land ownership, while they are all positive for the Northern village, confirming that the propensity to migrate is higher for individuals from households with large land ownership, they are not significant for the migration decision. Thus, the decision of migration is not significantly different for individuals belonging to different classes of land ownership. Land ownership in the Northern region is normally of smaller size than in Gezira, and as the estimates show is not as significant in influencing migration as in Gezira. However, for the latter it is noted that an individual with a

174

primary level of education from a household with large land ownership is less likely to migrate. With a possibility of staying unemployed in the urban area for a long period of time at a high opportunity cost, as the individual has the alternative to work in his family's land, a decision to move to the urban areas may not be worthwhile.

The high secondary and university level of education interaction with land is much more significant for Gezira village than the Northern village and for Gezira the interaction between secondary level and landownership is significantly different from zero. Thus, those with a high education level from households with large land ownership are encouraged to migrate. A consequence of this migration might be an aggravation of income inequality through income transfers.

Table (2): Maximum likelihood Estimate of the Migration Response Function

Covariate	All sample		Gezira		Northern	
	Coefficient	Marginal Effect	Coefficient	Marginal Effect	Coefficient	Marginal Effect
Age	.2316*	.0262*	.3412*	.0129*	.1904*	.0295*
	(9.72)	(8.54)	(7.31)	(2.86)	(6.56)	(6.31)
Age Square*10^{-2}	-.2772*	-.0314*	-.4255*	-.0161*	-.2192*	-.0340*
	(-8.50)	(-7.93)	(-6.62)	(-2.87)	(-5.53)	(-5.48)
Male	1.123*	.1273*	1.884**	.0714*	.9048*	.1405*
	(9.10)	(8.41)	(5.65)	(3.43)	(6.32)	(6.14)
Education						
Primary	.7985*	.0905*	.9583*	.0363**	1.051*	.1632*
	(3.60)	(3.38)	(2.26)	(1.68)	(3.47)	(3.41)
Junior Secondary	1.187*	.1345*	1.161*	.0440**	1.398*	.2170*
	(4.94)	(4.43)	(2.42)	(1.74)	(4.32)	(4.14)
High Secondary	.9984*	.1132*	.7102***	.0269***	1.196*	.1856*
	(4.32)	(3.95)	(1.60)	(1.34)	(3.81)	(3.68)
Tertiary	1.439*	.1631*	.1985	.0075	2.117*	.3286*
	(4.25)	(3.85)	(0.19)	(0.19)	(4.69)	(4.26)
Income						
Agricultural Income per adult*10^{-2}	-.0601*	-.0068*	-.0673*	-.0025*	-.0605*	-.0094*
	(-4.83)	(-4.85)	(-2.95)	(-2.18)	(-3.85)	(-4.10)
Non-agricultural Income per adult*10^{-2}	-.0069***	-.0008***	-.0394**	-.0015***	-.0044	-.0007
	(-1.29)	(-1.28)	(-1.83)	(-1.56)	(-0.80)	(-0.79)
Land owned per adult	-.0575	-.0065	-.0989	-.0037	-.0317	-.0049
	(-0.82)	(-0.83)	(-1.05)	(-1.04)	(-0.24)	(-.24)
Regional Dummy	-.0681	-.0077				
	(-0.66)	(-0.66)				
Education*Land						
Primary*land	.1312**	.0148**	-.0050	-.0002	.1065	.0165
	(1.83)	(1.88)	(-0.04)	(-0.04)	(0.80)	(0.81)
Junior secondary*land	.1217**	.0138**	.0966	.0036	.0983	.0152
	(1.68)	(1.73)	(0.71)	(0.71)	(0.74)	(0.74)

High secondary*land	.1279** (1.78)	.0145** (1.83)	.2082*** (1.62)	.0078*** (1.50)	.1029 (0.77)	.0159 (0.78)
Tertiary*land	.1575* (2.02)	.0178* (2.10)	.2678 (1.03)	.0101 (1.00)	.1273 (0.92)	.0197 (0.93)
Constant	-6.472* (-13.3)	-.7336* (-9.85)	-8.655* (-9.18)	-.3281* (-2.96)	-5.890* (-9.89)	-.9144* (-8.72)
R^2	0.63		0.73		0.62	
Log-likelihood	-421.		-153.		-253.	
Chi-Squared	404.		204.		222.	
Sample Size	1498		703		795	

Figures in parentheses are t-statistics.
* Significant at 5% level of significance.
** Significant at 10% level of significance.
*** Significant at 20% level of Significance.

5.Summary:

The empirical evidence of the estimated migration response function indicated that individuals in farming households who attained high education levels are more likely to migrate; and that, depending on the education level attained, an increase of 9%-6% in migration probability is expected for those who are educated (the incidence of migration among individuals aged 15 years and over ranged between 12%-17%).

Household land ownership influences migration negatively, with an increasing incidence of migration for individuals from households having low land/labor ratio, but the effect is not statistically significant. However, income per capita from agricultural output seems to be important and significantly influence decisions to migrate, with those individuals expecting higher per capita income from land being less likely to migrate. Nonetheless, individuals with high levels of education coming from families with large landholdings are encouraged to migrate. This effect might aggravate future income inequalities through income transfers of migrants.

Notes:

1. For the theoretical treatment see for example M. P. Todaro, "A model of Labor Migration and Urban Unemployment in Less Developed Countries," American Economic Review 59, no. 2 (1969): 138-48; J. R. Harris and M. P. Todaro, "Migration, Unemployment and Development: A Two-Sector Analysis," American Economic Review 60, no. 1 (1970): 126-42; G. E. Johnson, "The Structure of Rural Urban Migration," Eastern African Economic Review, (June 1971): 21-28; J. E. Stiglitz, "Rural urban Migration, Surplus labor and the Relationship between Urban and Rural Wages," Eastern African Economic Review, (1969): 1-28, "Alternative Theories of Wage Determination and Unemployment in LDC's: The Labor Turnover Model," Quarterly Journal of Economics 88, no. 12 (1974): 194-227; G. Fields, "Rural-Urban Migration, Urban Unemployment and Job Search Activity in L. D. C's," Journal of Development Economics 11, no.1 (1975): 47-53; A summary of the main issues and debate can be found in M. P. Todaro, Internal Migration in Developing Countries (Geneva: ILO, 1976). Examples of empirical work are: H. Barnum and R. H. Sabot, Education, Employment Probabilities and Rural-Urban Migration in Tanzania (Washington: IBRD, 1975); M. E. Levy and W. J. Wadycki, "Education and The Decision to Migrate: An Econometric Analysis of Migration in Venezuela," Econometrica 42 (March 1974): 377-88; G. S. Sahota, "An Economic Analysis of Internal Migration in Brazil," Journal of Political Economy 76,no. 2(March/April 1968):218-45; for estimation of migration decision functions see T. P. Schultz, "Notes on the Estimation of Migration Decision Functions," in Migration and the Labor Market in Developing Countries, ed. Richard H. Sabot (Colorado: Westview Press, 1982). pp.91-126.

2. See Todaro and J. R. Harris and M. P. Todaro (n.1 above).

3. J. R. Harris and M. P. Todaro (n.1 above).

4. See G. Fields (n.1 above).

5. The land area for Gezira measures only area of cotton land, the minimum of which is 5 feddans per tenant. In addition to this the farmers cultivate another 5 feddans with staple food and fodder. Feddan= 0.420 hectares (= 1.038 acres).

6. See G.S. Maddala, Limited-Dependent and Qualitative Variables in Econometrics (Cambridge: Cambridge University Press,1983).

7. This is $\delta P_i/\delta x_{ij} = \beta_j\ \varphi(Z_i)$, where $\varphi(.)$ is the density function of the standard normal.

8. See L. A. Sjaastad, "The Costs and Returns to Human Migration," Journal of Political Economy,Supp.70, no. 5(October 1962): 80-92.

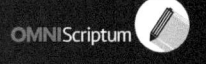